Women with ADHD

A Holistic, Practical and Actionable Approach to Embracing Your Uniquely Spectacular Brain

Kayla Farr

© Copyright Kayla Farr 2024

All rights reserved.

The content within this book may not be reproduced, duplicated or transmitted without direct written permission from the author or the publisher.

Under no circumstances will any blame or legal responsibility be held against the publisher, or author, for any damages, reparation, or monetary loss due to the information contained within this book. Either directly or indirectly. You are responsible for your own choices, actions, and results.

Legal Notice:

This book is copyright protected. This book is only for personal use. You cannot amend, distribute, sell, use, quote or paraphrase any part, of the content within this book, without the consent of the author or publisher.

Disclaimer Notice:

Please note the information contained within this document is for educational and entertainment purposes only. All effort has been expended to present accurate, up-to-date, and reliable, complete information. No warranties of any kind are declared or implied. Readers acknowledge that the author is not engaging in the rendering of legal, financial, medical or professional advice. The content within this book has been derived from various sources. Please consult a licensed professional before attempting any techniques outlined in this book.

By reading this document, the reader agrees that under no circumstances is the author responsible for any losses, direct or indirect, which are incurred as a result of the use of the information contained within this document, including, but not limited to, — errors, omissions, or inaccuracies.

Book Cover by Kayla Farr

1st edition 2024

Contents

Dedication	1
Acknowledgments	2
Introduction	5
1. Understanding Your ADHD	9
2. Emotional Regulation & Self-Esteem	17
3. Time Management & Organization	29
4. Enhancing Focus & Productivity	39
5. Building Healthy Relationships	45
6. Career & Professional Life	53
7. Holistic Health & Well-Being	63
8. Parenting with ADHD	91
9. Financial Management	101
10. Navigating Sensory Overload	109
11. Embracing Your ADHD Superpowers	117
Conclusion	127
You've Got This!	131
References	133

Dedication

To the incredible women who struggle with ADHD:

This book is for you—the ones who have felt misunderstood, overwhelmed, or do not quite fit in. You are not broken. You are brilliant, resilient, and uniquely spectacular.

May this journey help you embrace every part of yourself and remind you that your differences are your greatest strengths.

You are more than enough, just as you are. Keep going—you've got this.

Acknowledgments

Michael: Thank you for your love, patience, and unwavering support over the past ten years. I could not have done this without you by my side, always encouraging me to keep going. Never once have you questioned my ability, and you never doubted that I could do what I put my mind to. That is the kind of support I pray all our children find in a partner. You are loyal and true, my rock and my safe place. I love you. PS - You are also hilarious and smoking hot.

Delilah, Josephine, Madeline, and Owen: Thank you for your love and uncontainable joy. I apologize for the many sacrifices you made before I understood how my ADHD affected your lives. Your understanding means the world to me, and your love is the light of my life. May I continue to grow in love and light so that your childhoods will become inextinguishable embers of love and hope, constantly igniting your souls as you journey through life. Remember, darkness cannot remain in the light, fear cannot remain in love, and you create your own destinies.

Mom: You taught me to believe that I could do anything. I would have tried to be an astronaut if it had seemed interesting enough. I have never carried self-doubt about any skill-related thing, and I have you to thank for that. I love you.

Dad: You taught me (and all your daughters) how to be a man, instilling independence, dedication, hard work, and sacrifice. Thank you for showing me how to navigate life rather than sheltering me from it. I love you.

Emily, Katie, Kristen, and Dillon: Thank you for always believing in me, no matter how wild my dreams seemed. Your constant support pushed me to follow through on those dreams.

Dillon, here's an extra shout-out for confirming my ADHD self-diagnosis and for teaching me how ADHD affects men. Your knowledge and insights made a big difference. I know that I can always talk to you when things get rough.

Katy: Thank you for always stepping up and caring for our family, giving me the space and time to work on this book. I truly couldn't have done it without your help.

Big Bill: Thank you for being my sounding board throughout this journey of self-discovery. You never judged me; instead, you encouraged me to reach higher and keep exploring. You never once considered me a lunatic. Thanks for that.

Joseph, Jim, Little Bill, Sam, Pearson, Nanny Barb, and Grandma Debbie: You are the best family anyone could ask for, always offering to help and support when needed. And to the rest of my family—my aunts, uncles, and cousins—thank you for consistently rallying to our aid whenever we needed you.

I want to thank Rasmus and Christian Mikkelsen, especially for showing me the clearest path to achieving my dream of becoming a publisher.

Finally, thank you, dearest reader, for taking a chance on me and reading this book. I bless you and thank you a thousand times over.

This book exists because of all of you. I thank you with all of my heart.

Introduction

I stood in my kitchen a few years ago, staring blankly at a half-made sandwich. The bread was out, the cheese unwrapped, yet I couldn't remember what I had done moments before. I'd found myself lost in the middle of a simple task before. It was a moment that many of you might recognize—feeling overwhelmed by the smallest of chores, not because they are complex, but because our brains are wired differently.

You see, I have ADHD. Learning this about myself was both a relief and a revelation. Suddenly, so many of my struggles made sense. Still, it also meant facing the reality of living with a condition that often felt like it controlled my life. This book is born from that experience. I detail my journey to understanding the uniqueness of my brain and embracing the spectacular opportunities it affords.

The primary purpose of this book is simple. I aim to offer practical solutions for women struggling with ADHD symptoms. I want to encourage you to see ADHD not as a hindrance but as a gift. By focusing on ADHD's advantages, we can reshape our narratives and live fuller, more balanced lives.

What makes this book different is its holistic approach. We won't just discuss time management or organizational skills, though those are important. We'll also explore emotional regulation, relationships, and self-care. ADHD affects many parts of our lives, so our strategies must be just as comprehensive. This book will integrate various aspects of life affected by ADHD, providing a well-rounded approach to managing and embracing it.

You are the focus of this book. Whether you have just been diagnosed with ADHD or have long suspected it, whether you seek personal growth or are a professional or caregiver, this book is for you. It aims to reach women who are experiencing emotional challenges related to ADHD, making them feel seen and understood.

The book is organized into critical chapters, each addressing a different aspect of living with ADHD. We will start with understanding the basics of ADHD, followed by strategies for emotional regulation and time management. We will then explore how ADHD affects relationships and self-care. Each chapter builds on the previous one, giving you a clear roadmap.

Throughout the book, we will explore key themes such as embracing neurodiversity, leveraging ADHD traits as strengths, and finding practical solutions for daily challenges. A strengths-based approach is vital. We will use real-life examples and exercises to make these concepts relatable and actionable.

I am passionate about helping adult women overcome ADHD symptoms and achieve a balanced, fulfilling life. My background in project management and years of running a household have given me the insights needed to overcome the daily challenges you face with my easy-to-follow action steps. My personal experiences with ADHD add a layer of authenticity and empathy to my advice.

Reading this book, you can expect to gain practical tools, relatable stories, and simple strategies you can implement daily. The goal is to empower and support you on your journey as you transition from barely surviving to truly thriving with ADHD. This book is designed to be accessible and engaging, catering to your unique needs.

As you turn the pages, I encourage you to approach this book with an open mind and a willingness to try new strategies. You might find that some methods work perfectly for you while others don't. That's okay. The journey is about finding what fits your life and helps you shine.

Let me leave you with this thought. Your brain is uniquely spectacular. ADHD is a part of who you are, but it isn't your entire definition. It can be a source of creativity, energy, and passion. Embrace this journey of self-discovery and growth with excitement and hope. Together, we will uncover the gifts that ADHD brings and use them to create a life that feels balanced and fulfilling. Welcome to your new adventure.

Chapter 1
Understanding Your ADHD

Years ago, I found myself in a crowded grocery store, my cart half-full, yet I couldn't remember what I came for. The fluorescent lights buzzed overhead, adding to the cacophony of voices and the beeping of registers. I felt a wave of frustration and confusion wash over me, a sensation you might know all too well. It wasn't just about forgetting a shopping list; it was the overwhelming sense that I couldn't keep up with the simplest tasks. My experience wasn't an isolated incident but a recurring theme that echoed throughout my life. It was only much later that I came to understand these moments were part of living with ADHD, a revelation that changed everything.

The Unique ADHD Journey of Women

ADHD often presents differently in women compared to men, leading to a significant underdiagnosis or late diagnosis. Society expects women to be organized, nurturing, and emotionally stable. These gender roles can obscure the signs of ADHD, as women often internalize their struggles. While boys might exhibit hyperactive behaviors, girls with ADHD are more likely to display inattentiveness or internalized symptoms like daydreaming or anxiety. This discrepancy means many women grow up misdiagnosed or undiagnosed, their symptoms mistaken for anxiety or depression. They learn to mask their difficulties, developing coping mechanisms that hide their ADHD but at a significant emotional cost.

The emotional toll of undiagnosed ADHD is profound. Many women with ADHD feel a deep sense of inadequacy and self-doubt. They often compare themselves unfavorably to their peers, wondering why seemingly simple tasks are so challenging. This constant comparison leads to chronic stress and burnout. Struggling to meet societal expectations can result in the development of additional chronic conditions like anxiety and depression. The effort to appear "normal" is exhausting and can leave women feeling isolated and misunderstood.

My self-diagnosis occurred only within the past year, at 31 years old. I was researching how to help my oldest daughter learn to master executive function skills. While reading the AMAZING book "Smart But Scattered: The Revolutionary Executive Skills Approach to Helping Kids Reach Their Potential" by Peg Dawson and Richard Guare, I realized I also struggled with MANY of the discussed items. Time blindness? Check. Hyperfocus? Check. Anxiety? Check. Overstimulation? Double Check! Emotional Dysregulation? Triple Check! The revelation astounded me, and I went directly to my brother-in-law for more information. Dillon has been diagnosed with ADHD since his early childhood. He quickly confirmed exactly what I thought. I have struggled with ADHD my entire life without realizing that was the case.

Somehow, I have managed to stay ahead of ADHD for the most part, learning skills along the way by necessity to ensure I didn't lose my job, especially since project management has been my entire career (ironic, right???). However, after the unexpected birth of twins, a total hit to our finances, and a reintroduction to the workforce, life was kicking my butt. I know it's a cliché, but I genuinely felt like a ticking time bomb. I never knew when I was going to lose it. Every day was tough to navigate as I felt bogged down with responsibility. Self-diagnosis was such an immense relief. I always felt like I had a terrible, ugly monster living inside me, and I couldn't figure out how to get it out. I never felt like I could be myself without being judged or misunderstood. My lack of emotional control has always been a source of deep shame and regret. Understanding that I didn't have the proper tools and training to navigate life with these challenges helped me heal in a way that can't be explained. I imagine you know exactly what I'm talking about.

I haven't pursued an actual diagnosis from a doctor because I have lived with this for three decades. I know what it is (as anyone with ADHD can attest). I also do not intend to take prescription medication since I have found phenomenal holistic ways to manage my own ADHD symptoms. Please know that I am not against prescribed stimulants or pursuing a formal diagnosis from your doctor. Every woman's ADHD symptoms and journey is so unique. **You know you best.** I may pursue my own formal diagnosis in the future, but I have honestly been too busy to self-advocate with a doctor when there is lower-hanging fruit I can grasp on my own to navigate ADHD successfully. Plus, I tend to be impatient and don't like waiting on anyone, so there is that as well... LOL!

Awareness and education about ADHD in women are crucial. Healthcare professionals are beginning to recognize the unique ways ADHD manifests in women. This includes understanding the internalized symptoms and the impact of societal expectations. Self-advocacy is also vital. Women must feel empowered to seek help and speak up about their experiences. Resources such as books, support groups, and online communities can provide valuable information and support. By fostering a greater understanding of ADHD in women, we can create a more supportive environment that acknowledges and addresses their unique challenges.

Hormonal Influences on ADHD: Menstruation, Pregnancy, and Menopause

ADHD symptoms are not static; they ebb and flow, often influenced by hormonal changes throughout a woman's life. Estrogen, a primary hormone, plays a significant role in cognitive functions. It affects neurotransmitters like dopamine, serotonin, and norepinephrine, which are closely linked to attention and mood. When estrogen levels are high, attention and executive functioning skills can improve. Conversely, when estrogen drops, ADHD symptoms can worsen. This fluctuation is evident during different stages of life, from the menstrual cycle to pregnancy and menopause.

During the menstrual cycle, many women notice that their ADHD symptoms wax and wane. The hormonal rollercoaster can make the last two weeks of the cycle particularly challenging. Progesterone levels rise, and estrogen levels fall, leading to increased inattention, mood swings, and irritability. For me, it's like living with two sets of ADHD symptoms—one set that's relatively manageable, even advantageous at times, and another that feels overwhelming. Recognizing this pattern can be the first step in managing these fluctuations more effectively.

Pregnancy introduces another layer of complexity. During the first trimester, increased progesterone can exacerbate ADHD symptoms. Many women also discontinue their stimulant medications during pregnancy, leading to a noticeable decline in their ability to manage symptoms. Navigating through pregnancy with ADHD requires a thoughtful approach. Mindfulness techniques, such as meditation and deep-breathing exercises, can help manage stress and improve focus. Dietary adjustments can support brain health. Tracking symptoms correlating to hormonal changes can also provide valuable insights, helping to anticipate and prepare for challenging periods.

Menopause, marked by a significant decline in estrogen, often intensifies ADHD symptoms. Women report increased memory fog, difficulty focusing, and heightened emotional sensitivity. These changes can feel like a second adolescence, with the added responsibilities of adulthood. Understanding the impact of menopause on ADHD is crucial for managing these symptoms effectively. Gynecologists and endocrinologists often recommend hormone replacement therapy (HRT) to stabilize estrogen levels, though this isn't suitable for everyone. Consulting with healthcare providers can help determine the best course of action.

Dr. Patricia Quinn, an ADHD specialist, emphasizes recognizing these hormonal influences. "Hormones play a pivotal role in the lives of women with ADHD. Understanding these fluctuations can help women better manage their symptoms and improve their quality of life." Studies support this insight, highlighting the need for tailored ADHD management strategies that consider hormonal changes.

Personal Symptom Tracker Exercise

Create a personal symptom tracker to monitor how hormonal changes affect your ADHD symptoms. Include columns for dates, menstrual cycle phases, symptom intensity, and any notable triggers or stressors. After a few cycles, patterns will emerge, providing valuable insights for managing your symptoms.

Understanding the impact of hormonal changes on ADHD is empowering. It equips you with the knowledge to anticipate and manage symptoms, improving your overall well-being. You can confidently navigate these fluctuations by tracking symptoms, practicing mindfulness, and making dietary and lifestyle adjustments. The journey through menstruation, pregnancy, and menopause with ADHD is unique, but with the right strategies, it can also be manageable.

Late Diagnosis: Discovering ADHD in Adulthood

Many women are not diagnosed with ADHD until adulthood, often because their symptoms are misinterpreted or overlooked. In childhood, girls are expected to be quiet, attentive, and well-behaved, which can lead to their ADHD symptoms being mistaken for anxiety or depression. Gender stereotypes and societal expectations play a significant role in this mislabeling. Girls who daydream in class or struggle to stay organized might be seen as inattentive or absent-minded rather than as individuals with ADHD. This misinterpretation persists into adulthood as women continue to internalize their symptoms, masking their struggles and developing coping mechanisms that hide the true nature of their condition.

The lack of awareness about ADHD in adult women further compounds the problem. Many healthcare professionals do not have the required training to recognize ADHD in women, leading to misdiagnosis and inadequate treatment. Women with ADHD often hear that their symptoms are simply stress or anxiety. This misdiagnosis can delay proper treatment and support, leaving women to struggle with unmanaged symptoms for years. The emotional and psychological impact of such a late diagnosis is profound. Women often feel a mix of relief and grief upon learning they have ADHD. Relief comes from finally understanding the root of their struggles, while grief stems from the realization of missed opportunities and years spent battling an invisible foe.

Seeking a diagnosis can be daunting, but it is a crucial step towards better self-understanding and management. The first step is to find a healthcare professional experienced in diagnosing and treating ADHD in adults. This might be a psychiatrist, psychologist, or primary care physician with specialized training. The evaluation process typically involves a detailed history of symptoms, a physical examination, and possibly questionnaires or standardized tests. An accurate diagnosis opens the door to various treatment options, including medication, therapy, and lifestyle changes. The benefits of getting diagnosed extend beyond symptom management. It can lead to a profound shift in self-perception, replacing self-blame with self-compassion.

Navigating the emotional aftermath of a late diagnosis requires time and support. Many women experience feelings of loss and regret, mourning the years they spent struggling without understanding why. Processing these emotions is essential. Practicing self-compassion and acceptance can help in this healing process. Building a support network of friends, family, or support groups can provide the emotional backing needed during this time. It is also important to give oneself grace and patience, recognizing that adjusting to this new understanding of oneself takes time.

Moving forward after a diagnosis involves integrating this new understanding into daily life. Creating a personalized ADHD management plan can be incredibly beneficial. This plan might include medication, therapy, and practical strategies for managing symptoms. Accessing resources such as support groups and online communities can provide additional support and information. Setting realistic goals and expectations is also vital. Celebrating small victories and progress is essential rather than focusing solely on the challenges.

The journey towards understanding and managing ADHD in adulthood can be challenging, but it is also empowering. With the proper support and strategies, women can learn to embrace their ADHD, leveraging it as a unique aspect of their identity. This process involves not only practical changes but also a shift in mindset—viewing ADHD not as a deficit but as a part of what makes each woman uniquely spectacular.

Embracing Neurodiversity: Celebrating Your ADHD Brain

The concept of neurodiversity offers a powerful way to understand and appreciate the differences in our brains. Neurodiversity is the idea that neurological differences, like ADHD, autism, and dyslexia, are natural variations in the human genome. Rather than viewing these differences as deficits or disorders, the neurodiversity movement reframes them as unique traits that can contribute positively to society. This shift in perspective began in the late 20th century and has gained momentum, promoting the idea that diversity in brain function is just as important as ecosystem biodiversity. Embracing neurodiversity means recognizing that our brains' unique wiring can lead to innovative thinking, creative solutions, and diverse ways of experiencing the world.

One of the most significant benefits of embracing neurodiversity is the empowerment it brings. When you start to see ADHD as a difference rather than a deficit, it opens up a world of possibilities. ADHD traits often include creativity and out-of-the-box thinking, allowing us to approach problems from unique angles. This creativity can lead to groundbreaking ideas and solutions that others might overlook. High energy and enthusiasm are other common traits, providing the drive and passion to pursue projects with intensity and commitment. Additionally, strong empathy and intuition often accompany ADHD, enabling us to connect deeply with others and understand their emotions and needs.

Consider the story of Trudie Styler, an actor and filmmaker who succeeded despite her ADHD. Trudie's creative approach and relentless energy allowed her to thrive in the demanding world of film and theater. Her ability to think outside the box and her empathy for the characters she portrayed brought authenticity and depth to her performances. Similarly, Sharon Wohlmuth, a Pulitzer Prize-winning photojournalist, discovered her ADHD later in life. Sharon leveraged her intuitive eye and creative vision to capture powerful, vibrant images that resonated with worldwide audiences. These women, and many others like them, demonstrate how harnessing ADHD traits can lead to remarkable success in various fields.

Journaling prompts for self-discovery can also be beneficial. Set aside time each day to write about your experiences with ADHD. Focus on how your traits have helped you in different situations. For example, you might reflect on when your high energy allowed you to complete a project ahead of schedule or when your empathy helped you support a friend in need. Journaling reinforces positive self-perception and provides a space for self-reflection and growth.

Embracing neurodiversity and celebrating your ADHD brain is about changing the narrative. It's about acknowledging the challenges while focusing on the unique strengths that ADHD offers. Recognizing and valuing these traits can transform your perspective and empower you to thrive. The stories of successful women with ADHD serve as a testament to the incredible potential that lies within each of us. As you continue this journey, remember that your brain is not a barrier but a bridge to new possibilities. Embrace your differences, celebrate your strengths, and let your uniquely spectacular brain shine.

Chapter 2

Emotional Regulation & Self-Esteem

P icture this: you're sitting at your desk, trying to focus on an important task, when suddenly, a wave of frustration hits you out of nowhere. Your heart races, your palms sweat, and you're overwhelmed by an intense urge to scream or cry. You know you need to calm down, but the emotions feel too powerful to control. This scenario might sound familiar if you have ADHD. Emotional regulation can be one of the most challenging aspects of living with ADHD, but there are effective tools to help manage these intense emotions. One such tool is Dialectical Behavior Therapy (DBT).

Managing Intense Emotions with DBT Techniques

Dialectical Behavior Therapy, or DBT, is a therapeutic approach developed by Dr. Marsha Linehan initially to treat borderline personality disorder. Over time, its effectiveness in managing intense emotions has led to its application in treating various conditions, including ADHD. DBT's focus on balancing acceptance and change sets it apart from other therapeutic approaches. DBT teaches you to accept your emotions as they are while also learning how to change behaviors that may be harmful or unproductive.

DBT is a subset of Cognitive Behavioral Therapy (CBT) and incorporates elements of mindfulness and acceptance. Unlike traditional CBT, which focuses primarily on changing thought patterns, DBT emphasizes validating emotions before attempting to change them. This validation is crucial because it acknowledges your feelings as real and significant, providing a foundation for further therapeutic work. The therapy usually involves group and individual sessions focusing on skill-based modules.

One of the core principles of DBT is mindfulness, which involves focusing on the present moment without judgment. Mindfulness practices can significantly help those with ADHD, as they promote awareness and acceptance of one's thoughts and feelings. Practicing mindfulness can be as simple as taking a few minutes to sit quietly and pay attention to your breath each day. When your mind wanders, gently bring your focus back to your breath. This practice can help you stay present and reduce the impact of distracting thoughts and intense emotions.

Another essential component of DBT is distress tolerance, which teaches you to manage high emotions without resorting to harmful behaviors. The TIPP method is a practical distress tolerance technique that stands for Temperature, Intense exercise, Paced breathing, and Paired muscle relaxation. When you feel overwhelmed, try holding a cold pack to your face or running your wrists under cold water to change your body's temperature. Engaging in intense exercises, like jumping jacks or running in place, can also help release built-up tension. Paced breathing involves taking slow, deep breaths to calm your nervous system, while paired muscle relaxation focuses on tensing and relaxing different muscle groups to reduce physical stress.

Emotion regulation is another key area addressed by DBT. This skill involves identifying and labeling your emotions, which can help you understand and manage them more effectively. Start by keeping a journal where you write down your feelings and the situations that trigger them. Note the intensity of your emotions and any physical sensations you experience.

Over time, this practice can help you recognize patterns and develop strategies to cope with your feelings before they become overwhelming.

Let's put some of these skills into practice. Begin with a mindful breathing exercise. Find a comfortable place to sit, close your eyes, and take a deep breath through your nose. Hold it for a moment, then slowly exhale through your mouth. As you breathe, focus on the sensation of the air entering and leaving your body. As you breathe in, feel your lungs expand, making your chest rise. As you breathe out, feel your lungs deflating as your chest drops. Try this exercise for five minutes each day to cultivate mindfulness. We will expand on mindfulness techniques later in the book as well.

Next, create a distress tolerance kit. Gather items that can help you manage high emotions, such as a cold pack, a stress ball, a favorite book, or calming essential oils. Keep this kit in an easily accessible place so you can use it to soothe yourself. Having a distress tolerance kit at your disposal can be a lifesaver during moments of intense stress or anxiety.

For emotion regulation, use journaling prompts to explore your feelings. Write about a recent situation that triggered a strong emotional response. Describe what happened, how you felt, and any physical sensations you noticed. Reflect on what you could do differently next time to manage your emotions more effectively. This journaling practice can provide valuable insights into your emotional patterns and help you develop better coping strategies.

DBT offers a comprehensive set of skills tailored to help you navigate the emotional landscape of ADHD. By incorporating mindfulness, distress tolerance, and emotion regulation techniques into your daily routine, you can gain greater control over your emotions and improve your overall well-being. These skills are not just theoretical; they are practical tools that you can use to enhance your daily life.

Overcoming Negative Self-Talk: Building Self-Compassion

Negative self-talk can be a relentless companion for women with ADHD, exacerbating symptoms and significantly impacting self-esteem. The voice in your head that criticizes and doubts is thunderous, convincing you that you are not good enough, smart enough, or capable. This internal monologue often stems from years of misunderstood behavior and frequent criticism from others and yourself. Common negative thought patterns include phrases like:

I'm so stupid!

Why can't I just get it together?

I'll never be able to do this.

These thoughts are not only unkind but also deeply damaging. Chronic self-criticism can lead to a cycle of low self-esteem and increased ADHD symptoms, making it harder to break free from these negative beliefs.

Understanding the principles of self-compassion can be a game-changer in overcoming negative self-talk. Self-compassion, a concept developed by Dr. Kristin Neff, involves treating yourself with the same kindness and understanding you would offer a friend. It comprises three main components: self-kindness, common humanity, and mindfulness.

Self-kindness: being gentle and supportive of yourself rather than harshly critical.

Common humanity: recognizing that everyone makes mistakes and experiences difficulties helps you feel less isolated in your struggles.

Mindfulness: observing your thoughts and feelings without judgment, allowing you to accept your experiences without being overwhelmed.

Practicing self-compassion can reduce the intensity of negative self-talk and improve your overall emotional well-being. Unlike self-pity, which involves wallowing in your difficulties, self-compassion encourages active steps toward self-care and understanding.

To cultivate self-compassion, start with simple exercises that help replace negative self-talk with kinder, more supportive thoughts. One effective exercise is writing a self-compassionate letter. Imagine you are writing to a dear friend experiencing the same struggles you face. Use compassionate and empathetic language to offer support and understanding. After writing the letter, read it aloud to yourself. This exercise can help shift your perspective and remind you of the importance of treating yourself with kindness. Dr. Kristin Neff explains that "self-compassion provides the emotional safety needed for us to admit our shortcomings, forgive ourselves, and make the changes necessary to grow." This insight highlights the transformative power of self-compassion in building a healthier self-perception.

Another helpful practice is mindful self-compassion meditation. Find a quiet place to sit and close your eyes. Take a few deep breaths to center yourself. As you breathe, silently repeat phrases like:

I speak kindly to myself.

I accept myself as I am.

I freely give myself the compassion I need to grow.

I show myself love and patience.

I allow myself grace for things in my control.

I surrender to things outside my control.

This meditation can help internalize feelings of self-compassion and reduce the impact of negative self-talk.

Daily self-affirmation practices can also play a crucial role in building self-compassion. Start each day by looking in the mirror and stating positive affirmations, such as:

I am competent and capable.

I feel worthy to live the life of my dreams.

I am doing my best, and that is more than enough.

I feel deep gratitude for the gifts of creativity, energy, and empathy that ADHD provides.

I love my unique brain.

These affirmations can counteract negative thoughts and reinforce a positive self-image. Consistency is critical, so make this practice a part of your daily routine. Over time, these positive affirmations replace the negative self-talk that once dominated your thoughts. You can also use the recorder app on your phone to record yourself speaking affirmations lovingly. Consider listening to the recordings right before bed and first thing in the morning because this is when your mind is most susceptible to influence.

It is also essential to recognize that not all the thoughts in your head are true. More importantly, most of the narrative in your mind could be lies. I humbly ask you to examine your mental narrative for one day. Write down recurring thoughts you experience in a notebook. Review the list of thoughts you have written down. Examine each thought and ask yourself the questions below:

Does this thought show me love?

Would I speak this way to my child, family member, or friend?

Does this thought empower me to reach my goals?

Having ADHD is beyond your control, but you can command the thoughts that you allow to play the role of "The Wizard of Oz" in your mind. Fling back the curtain, grab the megaphone, regain control, and get your thoughts in order. Conscious self-awareness is the first step to improving your life.

Now that you have examined your thoughts to identify negative self-talk, the next step is to be the gatekeeper of your mind. The next time you have one of the "I'm so stupid" thoughts, stop yourself and say, "No, that is a lie. I am not stupid. I have a unique brain that enables me to do remarkable things." Alternatively, you could just say, "Liar, liar, pants on fire!"

Okay, here is a gentle reminder. Do you remember when I asked you to have an open mind at the beginning of the book? This exercise is a perfect example. Will you feel silly doing this exercise? Yes, you most certainly will. Could people look at you funny? Yes, they definitely will. But does it matter? NO! You only need to worry about creating a better life for yourself. The first step is exclusively speaking to yourself in love. If someone looks at you, simply reply, "Sorry, my mind is currently under construction, and the foreman occasionally uses the megaphone to get everyone back on track," then walk away. It's as simple as that. Look at you, improving yourself and spreading joy to the family discussing your unusual behavior over their dinner table.

Incorporating self-compassion into your daily life can replace negative self-talk with supportive and understanding thoughts. This shift can improve your self-esteem and help you manage your ADHD symptoms more effectively. Remember, treating yourself with kindness and compassion is not just lovely; it is a powerful tool for emotional regulation and personal growth.

Strategies for Reducing Social Anxiety

Social anxiety can feel like an invisible barrier, keeping you from fully engaging in life. For women with ADHD, this anxiety often stems from a unique set of triggers. One of the most prevalent is the fear of judgment and rejection. You might worry about saying the wrong thing or being perceived as awkward. This fear can be paralyzing, making social situations feel like minefields. Difficulty following social cues adds another layer of complexity. ADHD can make reading body language, maintaining eye contact, or keeping track of conversation threads difficult. These challenges can leave you feeling out of sync with others, amplifying your anxiety. Being overwhelmed in social settings is another common issue. Crowded rooms, loud noises, and multiple conversations can quickly become too much to handle, leading you to avoid these environments altogether.

Cognitive-behavioral techniques offer practical strategies to manage and reduce social anxiety. Cognitive restructuring is one such technique that helps you challenge negative thoughts and replace them with more balanced perspectives. Start by identifying a negative thought, such as "Everyone thinks I'm weird." Examine the evidence for and against this belief. You might realize there's no concrete proof that others judge you harshly. Replace the negative thought with something more empowering, like "People are focused on their own lives, not judging me." Exposure therapy is another effective method. It involves gradually facing your social fears in a controlled manner. Begin with low-stress situations, like chatting with a friendly coworker, and slowly work up to more challenging scenarios. This gradual exposure helps desensitize you to social anxiety triggers, making them less intimidating over time. Social skills training can also be beneficial. Practicing fundamental social interactions, such as introducing yourself or making small talk, can boost your confidence and improve your social competence.

Implementing actionable tips can further help manage social anxiety. Preparing conversation starters can be a game-changer. Having a few go-to topics in mind, like asking about someone's weekend or discussing a recent event, can ease the pressure of thinking on the spot. Relaxation techniques before social events can also make a significant difference. Deep breathing exercises, progressive muscle relaxation, or even a few minutes of meditation can calm your nerves and prepare you for the interaction ahead. Setting small, achievable social goals can build your confidence incrementally. Instead of aiming to be the life of the party, set a goal to engage in one meaningful conversation. Celebrate these small victories as they contribute to building your social confidence over time.

On the day of my first "real" job interview, I remember sitting in my car, paralyzed and anxious. My heart was racing. I couldn't breathe. I knew I was going to fail miserably. I almost left without going into the interview. I put the keys in the ignition and put the car in reverse, but in my gut, I knew that if I could calm down, there was a good chance the job would be mine. This time in my life was way before I knew I had ADHD, but intuitively (we have that skill too!) I began taking deep breaths through my nose, holding it for a few seconds, and then blowing the air out of my mouth. I also started singing comforting songs in my head as I continued the breathing exercise. I finally began to calm down enough to breathe comfortably. My heart was still racing, but I managed to nail the interview and land my first professional job. Looking back, I am so thankful that I didn't drive away. I learned many invaluable skills on the job and met some remarkable people I still call friends.

Understanding your social anxiety triggers and implementing these strategies allows you to navigate social situations more quickly and confidently. Creating a checklist can help you prepare for social situations. Include items like conversation starters, relaxation techniques, and achievable social goals. Having a checklist can provide a sense of control and readiness, reducing anxiety. Combining cognitive-behavioral techniques, practical tips, and real-life success stories offers a comprehensive approach to managing social anxiety, empowering you to engage more fully in social interactions and build meaningful connections.

Reframing ADHD Traits as Strengths

ADHD often has unique strengths that can be incredibly beneficial when recognized and leveraged. Creativity and innovative thinking are among the most notable traits. Women with ADHD frequently approach problems from unconventional angles, leading to solutions that others might not consider. This out-of-the-box thinking can be a tremendous asset, whether you're brainstorming a new project at work or finding creative ways to manage household tasks. High energy and enthusiasm are other familiar attributes. While this energy can sometimes feel overwhelming, it can also drive you to accomplish tasks with vigor and passion. When channeled effectively, this enthusiasm can make you a dynamic force in any setting.

Additionally, strong empathy and emotional intelligence often accompany ADHD. Heightened sensitivity allows you to connect deeply with others, understand their emotions, and offer meaningful support. These traits can make you a compassionate friend, a supportive partner, and an influential team member.

To help you identify and celebrate your unique ADHD traits, try engaging in practical exercises designed to highlight these strengths. Start with a strengths inventory worksheet. List your positive qualities and instances when these traits have benefited you. Reflect on moments when your creativity led to a successful outcome or your energy helped you through a challenging task. This exercise can help you recognize the value of your unique abilities and encourage you to view them as assets. Reflective journaling prompts can also be beneficial. Set aside time each day to write about how your ADHD traits have positively impacted your life. Focus on specific situations and the strengths you exhibited. Journaling reinforces positive self-perception and provides a space for self-reflection and growth. Visualization exercises can further reinforce a positive self-image. Close your eyes and imagine yourself in a situation where your ADHD traits are celebrated and appreciated. Visualize using your creativity to solve a complex problem, your energy to lead a team, or your empathy to build strong relationships. These mental images create a powerful narrative that shifts your focus from the struggles of ADHD to the strengths it brings.

To apply these strengths in your daily life, consider practical ways to integrate them into various aspects of your routine. Use your creativity in problem-solving by brainstorming multiple solutions to a challenge and selecting the most innovative one. This approach can be instrumental in work settings, where creative solutions are often highly valued. Leverage your empathy to build strong relationships by actively listening to others and offering support when needed. Your ability to understand and connect with people can make you a valuable friend and colleague. Channel your energy into productive activities by setting specific goals and dedicating your enthusiasm to achieving them. Whether completing a project, pursuing a hobby, or staying active, your energy can drive you to accomplish great things.

Reframing ADHD traits as strengths is about changing lanes in our brains. When we no longer drive down Wallow with Me Way and take a U-turn onto Can't Stop Me Lane, our challenges fade away as we focus on the unique strengths that ADHD offers. Recognizing and valuing these traits can transform your perspective and empower you to thrive. As you continue this journey, remember that your brain is not a barrier but a bridge to new possibilities. Embrace your differences, celebrate your strengths, and let your uniquely spectacular brain shine. I'm talking about you, Turquoise VW Van!

Chapter 3
Time Management & Organization

Imagine this: You're at your desk, ready to dive into a project, but before you know it, hours have passed, and you haven't even started. Instead, you are lost in a whirlwind of emails, social media, and random tasks. Time has slipped through your fingers without you even realizing it. This phenomenon, known as time blindness, is a common struggle for women with ADHD. It's about more than losing track of time; it's about being unable to sense how much time has passed or estimate how long tasks will take. Time blindness can lead to chronic lateness, missed deadlines, and a constant feeling of playing catch-up.

Time Blindness: Techniques to Improve Time Perception

Time blindness affects individuals with ADHD by distorting their perception of time. It makes estimating how long tasks will take difficult, leading to underestimations that result in rushed or incomplete work. You might think a task will only take 15 minutes when it takes an hour. This misjudgment can cascade into a series of delays, causing you to fall behind schedule. Being engrossed in an activity can lead to losing track of time altogether. You might start working on something and suddenly realize that hours have flown by, neglecting other important tasks. This tendency to hyperfocus on activities that capture your interest can be both a blessing and a curse.

Time blindness can also significantly impact punctuality and deadline adherence. You might find yourself consistently late to appointments or struggling to meet deadlines because you fail to properly judge how long it takes to get ready or complete tasks. Your shortcomings can strain relationships and affect your professional reputation.

Time blindness is closely linked to executive dysfunction, a common trait in ADHD. Executive functions are cognitive processes that help you plan, organize, and manage time efficiently. When these functions are impaired, it becomes challenging to gauge time accurately, prioritize tasks, and stick to schedules. This can lead to a constant sense of chaos and overwhelm.

Practical tools and techniques can make a significant difference in improving time perception. Visual timers and clocks are incredibly helpful. Placing a visual timer on your desk or using a clock with a countdown feature can provide a constant visual reminder of time passing. Seeing the time tick down can create a sense of urgency and help you stay on track. Setting specific time blocks for activities is another effective strategy. Allocate dedicated time slots for different tasks throughout your day. For example, set aside 30 minutes for checking emails, an hour for focused work, and 15 minutes for a break. This method helps create structure and prevents tasks from bleeding into each other. Regular time-checking intervals can also improve time perception. Set alarms or reminders to check the time regularly, such as every 30 minutes. This habit can help you know how much time has passed and adjust your pace accordingly.

Practical Exercise: Task Duration Estimation

Time-tracking logs for daily activities can provide valuable insights. Keep a log of how you spend your time each day, noting each activity's start and end times. Reviewing these logs can reveal trends and help you identify areas where time is lost. You can make adjustments to improve efficiency by understanding your time usage patterns. Comparing estimated versus actual time taken for tasks is another powerful exercise. Before starting a task, write down your estimated time. After completing it, record the exact time taken. Comparing these two figures can help you identify whether you're consistently underestimating or overestimating time. Over time, this practice can improve your ability to gauge time accurately.

Undeniably, this is one of the challenges I struggle with the most. If you were to spy on my family on any given weekend when I have convinced my husband to help me work on that "super easy DIY project," I'm sure you will see how I have optimistically estimated 2 hours. Fast-forward the tape four hours, and we are still finishing the raised garden beds. I do get the challenge that this presents. Thankfully, I am married to a realist who says, "We can give it a try," fully aware that he has just signed his entire Saturday over to me. Another option for gauging the amount of time a task should take is to ask others how much time they think it requires. After ten years of marriage, I have finally started asking my husband, "What is a reasonable amount of time to build the new compost bin?" and blocking that time off on our fridge calendar to finish the task.

Effective Task Management: The Power of Brain Dumps

Picture your mind as a cluttered desk overflowing with sticky notes, to-do lists, and random scraps of paper. This mental clutter can make it challenging to focus, prioritize, and get things done. Enter the concept of brain dumps, a simple yet powerful technique for managing overwhelming tasks and thoughts. A brain dump involves transferring all your thoughts, tasks, and worries from your mind onto paper or a digital medium. This process helps reduce mental clutter, making it easier to see what needs to be done and organize your tasks effectively.

Brain dumps offer several benefits. Externalizing your thoughts frees up mental space, allowing for greater clarity and focus. This method can also help alleviate anxiety by making your tasks more manageable. Writing everything down lets you see and break the big picture into smaller, actionable steps. Improved task management is a natural outcome of regular brain dumps, providing a clear roadmap for action steps and priorities.

Start by setting up the right environment to perform a brain dump effectively. Find a quiet, comfortable space where you won't be interrupted. Gather your materials, whether a notebook, a digital document, or an audio recording device. Begin by writing down every task, thought, and concern that comes to mind. Don't censor or organize your thoughts at this stage; the goal is to get everything out of your head and onto paper. Once you've captured all your thoughts, start organizing them into categories—group similar tasks together, such as errands, work-related tasks, or personal goals. Assign priorities to each task based on importance and urgency. This step helps you identify what needs immediate attention and what can wait.

Incorporating brain dumps into your daily life can make a significant difference in managing tasks and reducing stress. Schedule regular brain dump sessions, preferably at the start of the week. This habit helps you begin each week with a clear mind and a prioritized to-do list. You can also use brain dumps for specific projects. For instance, a brain dump can help you outline all the steps and tasks involved in planning a big event or working on a complex project. Decide whether you prefer digital or paper brain dumps. Some people find the tactile nature of writing on paper more satisfying, while others prefer the convenience and organization of digital tools. Choose the method that works best for you.

I have personally used brain dumps to manage my workload my entire career. Although they started as very unorganized lists (on pieces of paper that I continually lost), over time, I naturally began assigning priorities to my tasks to remain successful in my position. I have only recently implemented the priority matrix (discussed in more detail in Chapter 6) into my career. Still, it adds an often overlooked beneficial element for women who struggle with ADHD: visualization. The priority matrix has four quadrants to review to identify immediate action steps quickly. I can easily move on to what I have time to complete or feel the energy to accomplish. I cannot stress the sheer amount of mental clarity achieved through brain dumps. As my children age, I intend to implement the Priority Matrix for each of them to prevent being bombarded by "Mom, I need this" or "Mom, my teacher said that" as soon as I walk in the door. They can write down everything they need from me, and I can assign all the priorities simultaneously. This process can be as simple as putting a piece of paper in a basket or individual dry-erase boards hanging on the wall in the home command center.

Incorporating brain dumps into your daily routine can transform how you manage tasks and reduce stress. This simple yet effective technique helps you externalize your thoughts, prioritize tasks, and create a clear action plan. By freeing up mental space and reducing clutter, brain dumps provide a roadmap for managing your responsibilities and achieving your goals. It also empowers you to ask others for help by delegating tasks to coworkers, family members, and friends. Do you have a partner that doesn't pull their weight? Brain dump and ask them to take ownership of a task or two, dare I say three? Do you have a friend or family member always asking how they can help? Hand them your list and let them choose. Repeat this process regularly to maintain mental clarity and effective task management.

Simplifying Daily Routines with Practical Tools

Life with ADHD can often feel chaotic, as if you're constantly juggling too many balls at once. Simplifying your daily routines can make a world of difference. Streamlined routines reduce decision fatigue and the mental exhaustion of making too many choices. By creating consistent and predictable patterns in your day, you minimize the overwhelming feeling of chaos and anxiety. Simplified routines provide stability, making it easier to navigate your day confidently and easily.

One of the most effective ways to simplify your daily routines is by establishing morning and evening routines. A well-structured morning routine sets the tone for the day. Start with small, manageable tasks like making your bed, brushing your teeth, and having breakfast. These activities create a sense of accomplishment early on, boosting your motivation for the rest of the day. Stick to this routine every morning to create consistency. Use checklists and planners to keep track of your morning tasks. Write down each routine step and check them off as you go. This visual reminder helps you stay on track and ensures you overlook nothing.

Evening routines are equally important. They help you wind down and prepare for a restful night's sleep. Begin by setting a specific time to start your evening routine. This could be an hour before bedtime. Engage in calming activities like reading, practicing mindfulness, or taking a warm bath. Use checklists to ensure you complete necessary tasks such as setting out clothes for the next day, preparing your lunch, and tidying up your space. By creating a consistent evening routine, you signal to your body that it's time to relax, which can improve your sleep quality.

Automating repetitive tasks is another powerful tool for simplifying routines. Identify tasks that you perform regularly and find ways to automate them. For example, set up automatic bill payments to avoid the stress of remembering due dates. Input your recurring bills into your phone calendar to easily see when something is due or will be drafted from your bank account. Use subscription services for household essentials like groceries or cleaning supplies so you don't have to worry about running out. Utilize order pickup services for your groceries. Our household utilizes Walmart Grocery Pickup orders all the time. The beautiful thing about this is that you are usually getting the same items at the grocery store. Walmart creates lists of your previous purchases and offers suggestions. Thanks for remembering the milk! Automating these tasks frees up mental space and reduces the cognitive load, allowing you to focus on more critical activities.

Decluttering and organizing physical spaces also play a crucial role in simplifying routines. A cluttered environment can be overwhelming and distracting, making it harder to focus and complete tasks. Start by decluttering one area at a time. Remove items you no longer need or use, and find designated spots for everything else. Storage solutions like bins, shelves, and labels keep things organized. A tidy and organized space promotes a sense of calm and makes it easier to find what you need, reducing stress and saving time. Evaluating why you have so much clutter is also a good practice. Do you struggle with feelings of unworthiness or lack? Don't do all the work of cleaning your space just to fill it back up with things because you stress shop. Take the time to examine your motivations and behaviors. It's always worth the time investment.

Weekly planning sessions can enhance your routines by providing a clear roadmap for the week ahead. Set aside time each weekend to review your upcoming tasks and appointments. Use a planner or digital calendar to map your week, allocating specific time blocks for each activity. This practice helps you stay organized and pay attention to valued commitments. Monthly decluttering sessions are also beneficial. Dedicate one day each month to decluttering and organizing your space. Focus on one area at a time, such as your closet, kitchen, or workspace. Regular decluttering sessions prevent clutter from accumulating and maintain an organized environment.

As a busy, working mother of four (with three under three), I often feel overwhelmed by my daily household responsibilities. I finally decided to simplify my life by making a cleaning routine that I could maintain. I went to Walmart and purchased a weekly dry-erase board and a label maker. Then, I assigned cleaning tasks for each day of the week. We use cloth diapers for the twins, and with four children, the everyday laundry is constantly piling up. I alternated days for washing clothes and washing diapers. I assigned daily tasks of a 15-minute tidying, taking out the trash, and doing dishes. Then, I assigned rooms to clean each day. Mondays are for the kitchen. Tuesdays are laundry only, as we have recurring appointments. Wednesdays are for the living room. Thursdays are for bathrooms. Fridays are for bedrooms, the litter box, and watering my plants. Saturdays are for the mudroom. Sundays are only laundry as well.

I then posted this schedule right in the heart of my home, so I pass it often. I also put a daily reminder at 7:30 pm to do daily cleaning. So I perform the daily cleaning assignment and then do my 15-minute tidying of the entire house, putting things in their designated homes. I also encourage my children to participate in the 10-minute "Tidy Tornado," where we make a game of cleaning as quickly as possible. I set a visual descending timer for ten minutes. We all spun around three times, and then we saw who could tidy up most things before the timer went off. The spinning makes it silly, the timer makes it a competition, and best of all, they are learning how to contribute to a household. Is this system perfect? No. Do I always stick to it? Again, no. But having this schedule plastered to the wall where all my guests can see holds me accountable and motivates me to get up after a long day. I don't have to be overwhelmed about cleaning my entire house. It's Wednesday. I only need to clean the living room.

Simplifying your daily routines involves creating consistent patterns, using practical tools, and maintaining an organized environment. Establishing morning and evening routines, automating repetitive tasks, and decluttering your space can significantly reduce decision fatigue, minimize overwhelm, and create a sense of stability. Following these strategies makes it easier to manage your time and navigate your day confidently and efficiently.

Overcoming Procrastination: Small Steps to Big Success

Procrastination is a familiar obstacle for many women with ADHD. The underlying causes are often multifaceted. One such cause is the fear of failure and perfectionism. You may find yourself delaying tasks because you are afraid they won't meet your high standards. This fear can be paralyzing, making it difficult to start anything. Severe overwhelm and task paralysis are other significant factors. When faced with a daunting to-do list, you might feel so overwhelmed you can't decide where to begin. This paralysis can lead to avoidance, as tackling the tasks feels insurmountable. Difficulty with task initiation further complicates matters. Taking that first step can seem impossible despite knowing what needs to be completed. The executive dysfunction associated with ADHD makes it challenging to sequence and prioritize tasks, leaving you stuck in inaction.

Breaking tasks into smaller, manageable steps can effectively tackle procrastination. Imagine you have a big project to complete. Break it into smaller, bite-sized pieces instead of viewing it as one massive task. For example, if you need to write a report, start by outlining the main sections. Then, focus on writing one section at a time. This approach makes the task feel less overwhelming and more achievable. Setting specific and attainable goals can also help. Instead of aiming to "finish the report," set a goal to "write the introduction" or "research the first topic." These smaller goals are easier to accomplish and provide a sense of progress.

The "two-minute rule" is another practical strategy. The idea is simple: if a task takes less than two minutes, do it immediately. This rule helps you overcome the initial resistance to starting tasks. For instance, if you need to respond to an email or tidy up your desk, doing the task immediately prevents it from lingering on your to-do list. Rewarding progress and celebrating small wins is crucial for maintaining motivation. After completing a task, give yourself a small reward, like a short break or a treat. Celebrating these victories reinforces positive behavior and encourages you to keep going.

Daily goal-setting exercises can help you implement these strategies. Start each day by writing down three specific tasks you want to accomplish. Focus on setting realistic and achievable goals. Review what you achieved and celebrate your progress at the end of the day. Task breakdown worksheets can also be beneficial. Create a worksheet for each project, listing all the smaller tasks involved. Check off each task as you complete it, visually representing your progress. Two-minute task lists are another helpful tool. Write down all the tasks that can be completed in less than two minutes. Use this list to quickly knock out small tasks throughout the day, reducing the overall burden.

By understanding the connection between ADHD and procrastination and implementing practical strategies, you can overcome this common challenge. Breaking tasks into smaller steps, setting specific goals, using the two-minute rule, and celebrating small wins can help you take small steps toward big success. These strategies make tasks more manageable and build momentum and motivation, empowering you to achieve your goals.

This chapter explored techniques to manage time perception, task organization, routine simplification, and overcoming procrastination. Integrating these strategies into your life can create a more structured and less overwhelming daily routine. Next, we'll delve into enhancing focus and productivity, offering tools to help you thrive.

Chapter 4
Enhancing Focus & Productivity

One rainy morning, I found myself immersed in a sewing project for hours without noticing the time fly by. The outside world ceased to exist; it was just me, the fabric, and my sewing machine. This intense concentration felt like a superpower, a rare moment when my ADHD brain was entirely focused and productive. I was so in the grove that I worked through lunch without noticing hunger. If you've ever experienced this, you might be familiar with hyperfocus.

Harnessing Hyperfocus: Turning Passion into Productivity

Hyperfocus is when individuals with ADHD can concentrate intensely on a project or task for extended periods to the extent that everything else fades away. This phenomenon is not contradictory to ADHD but rather a critical manifestation. In hyperfocus, you might find yourself deeply engrossed in an activity, losing track of time and ignoring external distractions. This state often occurs when you're engaged in something that interests you, such as a hobby, a work project, or even a video game.

The benefits of hyperfocus include extreme productivity and the ability to improve skills through dedicated effort. Focused attention can help you accomplish significant achievements quickly and develop lasting friendships and romantic relationships. However, hyperfocus also has its drawbacks. It can lead to frustration for friends and family, who may find it difficult to break you out of this state. You might neglect responsibilities and chores and even ignore physical needs like eating and sleeping (#onemorechapter for all my book-loving gals).

To intentionally trigger hyperfocus, start by identifying passion projects and areas of interest. Reflect on activities that captivate your attention and make you lose track of time. These are the tasks where hyperfocus is most likely to occur. Setting specific goals and deadlines can also help. Clear objectives provide a sense of direction and purpose, making it easier to enter a state of hyperfocus. For instance, if you're passionate about writing, set a goal to complete a certain number of pages or chapters by a specific date. Creating an engaging and stimulating work environment is another crucial strategy. Surround yourself with items and tools that inspire you, such as artwork, motivational quotes, or music. A well-organized space can also minimize distractions and enhance your focus. Additionally, sensory tools like noise-canceling headphones or background music can help maintain concentration and block out external disruptions.

Managing hyperfocus requires a balance to avoid burnout and neglect of other responsibilities. Setting timers to take regular breaks is crucial. Use alarms or reminders to prompt you to step away from your task and recharge. These breaks can help prevent mental fatigue and maintain productivity over the long term. Balancing hyperfocus sessions with other activities is also essential. Schedule time for physical activity, social interactions, and self-care to ensure a well-rounded routine. This balance can help you stay energized and avoid the pitfalls of hyperfocus, such as neglecting your health or personal relationships.

By understanding and harnessing hyperfocus, you can turn this unique ADHD trait into a powerful tool for productivity and achievement. Identifying passion projects, setting clear goals, creating an engaging work environment, and balancing hyperfocus with other activities can help you maximize this intense concentration. These strategies enhance productivity and empower you to leverage your ADHD strengths for personal and professional success.

The Role of Body Doubling: Enhancing Focus with Support

Body doubling is a productivity strategy where another person works alongside you to help you stay focused and motivated. This method can be particularly beneficial for individuals with ADHD, who often struggle with staying on task due to impulsivity, distractions, and low motivation. The concept is simple: having a companion nearby provides a sense of accountability and support, making it easier to complete tasks. You cannot underestimate the psychological impact of having a body double present. It creates a sense of shared purpose and reduces feelings of isolation, which can be motivating and comforting.

To set up a successful body doubling partnership, choose the right body double. This person could be a friend, family member, or coworker who understands your needs and is supportive. Selecting someone who is nonjudgmental and can provide the right amount of interaction without becoming a distraction is indispensable. Once you've chosen your body double, set clear goals and expectations for your sessions. Discuss what you hope to achieve and how your body double can best support you. The approach might involve working silently side-by-side or occasionally checking in on each other's progress.

Scheduling regular body doubling sessions can help establish a routine. Consistency is key whether you meet daily, weekly, or as needed. If meeting in person isn't possible, consider using virtual platforms for remote body doubling. Video chat services like Zoom or FaceTime can replicate the feeling of having someone present, providing the same benefits as in-person sessions. Remote body doubling can be particularly useful for those who live far from their support network or have busy schedules.

Body doubling can be applied to various areas of life, from work tasks and projects to household chores and exercise. Having a body double for work tasks can help you stay focused on projects, complete assignments, and manage time more effectively. Partnering for household organization and cleaning can make these often tedious tasks more enjoyable and manageable. Imagine tackling a cluttered room with a friend by your side, working together, and keeping each other motivated. Using body doubling for exercise and fitness can also be beneficial. Working out with a partner can provide the motivation and accountability needed to stick to a fitness routine, making it easier to achieve your health goals.

Consider the story of Alejandra, a business owner who struggled with productivity. Alejandra found that working alongside her friend Tammy, a small business owner, significantly increased her output. They scheduled regular body doubling sessions at a local coffee shop, each focusing on their tasks. The presence of a supportive friend helped Alejandra stay on track and complete her to-do list more efficiently. Another example is Zara, a mother who found it challenging to keep her home organized. Zara's neighbor, Ashley, offered to help her with household chores once a week. They took turns working on each other's homes, making the process more enjoyable and less overwhelming. This partnership improved their homes and strengthened their friendship.

Incorporating body doubling into your routine can enhance your focus and productivity in various aspects of life. Choosing the right body double, setting clear goals, scheduling regular sessions, and using virtual platforms are practical steps to establish a successful partnership. Whether for work, household chores, or fitness, body doubling supports and motivates you to stay on track and accomplish your tasks.

Creating a Distraction-Free Environment

Your environment plays a crucial role in your ability to focus. Clutter and visual distractions can be overwhelming, making it difficult to concentrate on tasks. A messy desk or a room filled with unnecessary items can divert your attention from what you need to do. Visual chaos causes mental chaos, leading to a scattered mind. Noise and auditory distractions are equally problematic. Background chatter, loud noises, or even the hum of appliances can disrupt your focus. These sounds pull you out of your work, constantly forcing your brain to switch contexts. Digital distractions like notifications and social media are another major challenge. Every ping from your phone or pop-up on your computer screen is a temptation to divert your attention. These interruptions break your flow and make it difficult to regain focus.

Creating a distraction-free environment starts with decluttering and organizing your workspace. Begin by clearing your desk of non-essential items. Keep the tools that you need for the task at hand. Use storage solutions like bins, shelves, and drawer organizers to keep everything in its place. A clean, organized space promotes a sense of calm and makes it easier to focus. Noise-canceling headphones or white noise machines can help manage auditory distractions. These tools block out background noise, allowing you to concentrate on your work. Choose a calming instrumental music or white noise playlist to create a consistent auditory environment that supports focus.

Setting boundaries for digital device usage is crucial. Turn off non essential notifications on your phone and computer. Use apps that block distracting websites during work hours. Set specific times to check your email and social media rather than allowing them to constantly interrupt your workflow. These boundaries help you stay focused and minimize digital distractions.

For different environments, specific adjustments can make a significant difference. In a home office setup, position your desk away from high-traffic areas. Use a comfortable chair and ensure your lighting is adequate but not harsh. Keep your workspace dedicated to work-related activities, avoiding the temptation to use it for leisure. For a quiet study area at home, choose a location away from noisy appliances and common areas. Use bookshelves or partitions to create a physical barrier that signals a dedicated study space. Organize study materials in labeled folders and bins to make everything accessible and reduce visual clutter. In a creative space, ensure you have all the necessary tools and materials within arm's reach. Use pegboards, shelves, and containers to keep everything organized. A tidy, creative space lets you focus on your work without searching for materials.

Creating a distraction-free environment can significantly improve your ability to focus and complete tasks efficiently. Decluttering and organizing your workspace, using noise-canceling tools, and setting boundaries for digital device usage are practical steps to enhance your concentration. Whether working from home, studying, or engaging in creative pursuits, a distraction-free environment sets the stage for productivity and success.

As we conclude this chapter, remember that enhancing focus and productivity involves multiple strategies, from harnessing hyperfocus to creating distraction-free environments. These tools help you navigate the unique challenges of ADHD, leading to a more organized and fulfilling life. Next, we'll explore building healthy relationships, another crucial aspect of thriving with ADHD.

Chapter 5
Building Healthy Relationships

As I prepared dinner one evening, my partner and I started discussing our day. Within minutes, the conversation turned into a heated argument. I had interrupted him several times without realizing it. He felt unheard, and I felt misunderstood. This scenario is common for many women with ADHD. Communication in relationships can be a minefield, filled with misunderstandings and frustrations, mainly when ADHD symptoms are at play.

Communicating Effectively with Your Partner

Women with ADHD often face unique challenges in romantic relationships. One of the main issues is the tendency to interrupt or lose focus during conversations. This behavior isn't intentional; it results from the ADHD brain's difficulty regulating attention. You might jump in with your thoughts or get distracted by something else in the middle of your partner's sentence. This challenge can lead to feelings of frustration and resentment on both sides. Difficulty expressing your emotions is another challenge. You might struggle to articulate your feelings, leading to misunderstandings. Your partner might perceive your hesitance as disinterest or indifference, further straining the relationship. Misunderstandings and conflict stemming from ADHD symptoms are all too common. Your partner might misinterpret your forgetfulness as a lack of care or your impulsivity as thoughtlessness. These misunderstandings can create a cycle of conflict and hurt, making effective communication even more critical.

Improving communication in your relationship involves adopting practical strategies to enhance understanding and connection. Active listening exercises can be incredibly beneficial. This practice involves fully concentrating on your partner's words without planning your response or interrupting. Make eye contact, nod, and provide verbal acknowledgments like "I see" or "That's interesting." Active listening shows your partner that you are fully engaged and value their words. Using "I" statements to express feelings is another effective technique. Instead of saying, "You never listen to me," try, "I feel unheard when we talk." This approach focuses on your feelings rather than placing blame, making it easier for your partner to understand your perspective without becoming defensive. Setting aside regular time for focused discussions can also improve communication. Schedule "talk time" where you can discuss important issues without distractions. This dedicated time allows both of you to prepare mentally and emotionally, reducing the likelihood of misunderstandings.

Practicing communication skills can further strengthen your relationship. Role-playing common scenarios is a convenient exercise. For example, if you often argue about household chores, practice a conversation where you calmly discuss your expectations and listen to each other's concerns. This exercise can help you develop better communication patterns and understand each other's viewpoints. Communication check-ins are another valuable tool. Set aside time each week to check in with each other about how you're feeling and discuss any issues that have arisen. This regular check-in helps prevent minor problems from escalating into major conflicts. Journaling and sharing reflections can also enhance communication. Write down your thoughts and feelings about your relationship, then share them with your partner. This practice encourages open and honest dialogue, helping you understand each other's perspectives more deeply.

Consider the story of Emma and Jack, who struggled with constant arguments about their busy schedules. They decided to try active listening exercises. During their discussions, they consciously listened and acknowledged each other's points without interrupting. This change in their communication style helped them understand each other's challenges, reducing their conflicts. Another example is Sandra and Matthew, who used "I" statements to improve communication. Sandra often felt overwhelmed by household responsibilities, but instead of accusing Matthew of not helping, she expressed her feelings using "I" statements. "I feel stressed when the house is messy because it adds to my workload." This approach made Matthew more receptive to her concerns and willing to help.

By understanding the unique communication challenges in relationships with ADHD and implementing practical strategies, you can improve your connection with your partner. Active listening, using "I" statements, and setting aside time for focused discussions are effective techniques that can enhance understanding and reduce conflict. Practicing these skills through role-playing, communication check-ins, and journaling can further strengthen your relationship. Effective communication is the foundation of a healthy and fulfilling relationship, and with dedication and practice, you can build a stronger connection with your partner.

Navigating Friendships with ADHD

Building and maintaining friendships can be a daunting task for women with ADHD. One common challenge is forgetting important dates and events. You might have every intention of remembering a friend's birthday or attending a planned get-together, but the day slips by without a reminder. The tendency to forget important events can lead to guilt and frustration, not to mention disappointment from your friends. Another challenge is maintaining regular contact. Life gets busy, and before you know it, weeks have passed without a simple text or call to check in. This inconsistency can strain friendships, making it seem like you don't care when, in reality, your mind is just juggling too many things. Social settings can also be overwhelming, leading to avoidance. The noise, the crowd, and the constant stimulation can make social events feel like a sensory overload, pushing you to retreat rather than engage.

Despite these challenges, there are practical strategies you can adopt to nurture your friendships. Setting reminders for important dates can be incredibly helpful. Use your phone's calendar or reminder app to alert you a few days before a friend's birthday or a scheduled meet-up. This way, you have time to prepare and show your friends you value these moments. I would forget 75% of my family and friends' birthdays if it weren't for being programmed in my Google Calendar with reminders. And I'm still adding dates to this day (sorry, Tyler!).

Scheduling regular catch-up sessions is another effective strategy. Set a recurring monthly or bi-weekly date to call or meet with your friends. This consistency helps maintain the connection and shows your commitment to the friendship. Being open about your ADHD with friends can also make a significant difference. Explain that your forgetfulness or occasional distance isn't a sign of disinterest but a symptom of ADHD. Most friends will appreciate your honesty and be more understanding.

Managing social overwhelm is crucial for maintaining friendships. Planning and preparing for social events can make a big difference. If you know an event will be crowded or noisy, plan to arrive early when it's less busy and find a quieter spot to retreat if needed. Using relaxation techniques before and during interactions can help you stay calm. Deep breathing exercises or a brief meditation session can reduce anxiety and make social interactions more manageable. Setting boundaries is equally important. Know your limits, and don't be afraid to take breaks when you feel overwhelmed. Whether stepping outside for fresh air or finding a quiet room, taking a moment for yourself can help you recharge and re-engage.

To further help you navigate friendships, consider creating a social reminder checklist. Include important dates like birthdays and anniversaries, and set reminders a few days in advance. Schedule regular catch-up sessions with friends and note them on your calendar. Practice relaxation techniques like deep breathing or meditation before social events. And don't forget to communicate openly with your friends about your ADHD. Transparency can foster understanding and strengthen your relationships.

Building a Support Network

Having a solid support network is crucial for women with ADHD. Emotional support during challenging times is invaluable. Knowing someone is there to listen and offer empathy can make the difference between feeling overwhelmed and capable. Practical help with tasks and responsibilities is also essential. Whether it's a family member helping with household chores or a friend assisting with organizing your workspace, this practical support can alleviate some of your daily pressures. Feeling understood and less isolated is another significant benefit. Being surrounded by people who "get" you and your ADHD can be incredibly comforting and empowering. Be bold and bold and ask for help. You rob your friends and family of the deep joy of helping you when you refuse to ask or let them help you. Think of it this way: if your friend were in your shoes, you would already have the car halfway out of the driveway on the way to help them. Friends and family want to help. Ask and let them!

To build and maintain a support network, start by identifying potential supporters. Look around at your family, friends, and colleagues. Who are the people you trust and feel comfortable with? Make a list of these individuals. Next, reach out and express your needs. Communication can be as simple as saying, "I've been feeling overwhelmed lately and could use some help organizing my tasks." Being open about your needs allows others to understand how they can support you. Once you've identified your supporters, it's vital to nurture these relationships regularly. Stay in touch, show appreciation, and reciprocate support when you can. Relationships are a two-way street, and maintaining them requires ongoing effort.

Connecting with ADHD-specific support groups and communities can also provide invaluable support. Online forums and social media groups are great places to start. These platforms offer a sense of community and a space to share experiences and advice. Local support groups and meetups can provide face-to-face interaction and a more personal connection. Several online communities stand out for their supportive and resourceful environments. ADDitude Magazine's online forum is a treasure trove of discussions on various aspects of ADHD, from managing symptoms to navigating relationships. Reddit's ADHD Women community offers a space for shared experiences and advice specific to women with ADHD. Facebook groups like "Women with ADHD" provide peer support and a sense of camaraderie. Look for groups in your area that focus on ADHD support. Professional networks and organizations, such as CHADD (Children and Adults with Attention-Deficit/Hyperactivity Disorder), offer resources and connections to professionals who understand ADHD. These networks can provide both practical advice and emotional support.

I am extremely fortunate to have an extensive support group (hello acknowledgments page). Unfortunately, I spent most of my adult life refusing to let them help me. A lot changed when Mike and I found out that we would have twins, including me accepting that I wouldn't be Miss Independent anymore. I knew I would have to ask for help, and that admission grated on every fiber of my identity. I had to let go of the self-imposed belief that my family was my sole responsibility and that I shouldn't ask others to do "my job." Please don't impose ridiculous beliefs on yourself that set you up for burnout and failure. You are in the center of "community." Comm-U-nity. We are all the same and are meant to live in unity, lifting each other to greater heights.

Building a support network involves identifying potential supporters, reaching out and expressing your needs, and regularly nurturing these relationships. Connecting with ADHD-specific support groups and communities can provide additional support and understanding. By surrounding yourself with people who can offer emotional support, practical help, and a sense of experience, you can navigate the challenges of ADHD with greater confidence and resilience.

Handling Social Situations with Confidence

Social situations can be daunting for women with ADHD. Anxiety about social interactions is a common hurdle. You might worry about making a good impression or fear saying something awkward. This anxiety can be paralyzing, making it challenging to engage fully in conversations. Fear of judgment or rejection is another significant obstacle. The worry that others might judge you harshly or reject you can make social settings feel like a minefield. This fear often stems from past experiences where your ADHD symptoms were misunderstood or criticized. Difficulty following social cues and norms adds another layer of complexity. Picking up on subtle cues like body language, tone of voice, or the flow of conversation can be challenging. You might find yourself unintentionally interrupting or missing the mark on social norms, leading to embarrassment or frustration.

Boosting social confidence involves practicing social skills in low-pressure settings. Start by conversing with friends or family members who understand your ADHD. These low-stress interactions allow you to practice without the fear of judgment. Use these opportunities to work on maintaining eye contact, listening actively, and responding appropriately. Remember, you are listening to learn, not listening to respond. Positive self-talk and affirmations can also make a big difference. Before attending a social event, remind yourself of your strengths and past successes. Phrases like "I am capable of having meaningful conversations" or "I am valued for who I am" can boost your confidence. Setting achievable social goals is another practical strategy. Instead of aiming to be the life of the party, set smaller, more attainable goals like having one meaningful conversation or staying at the event for a certain amount of time. These goals provide a sense of accomplishment and build your confidence over time.

Improving social skills takes practice and dedication. Role-playing common social scenarios can be a helpful exercise. For example, practice introducing yourself, making small talk, or handling a disagreement with a friend or family member. This rehearsal can prepare you for real-life interactions and make you feel more confident. Attending social skills workshops is another great way to enhance your abilities. These workshops offer structured environments to practice social interactions and receive feedback. Look for local community centers, support groups, or online resources that offer such workshops. Practicing active listening and conversation starters can also improve your social skills. Focus on genuinely listening to the other person, asking open-ended questions, and showing genuine interest in their responses. Having a few go-to conversation starters can help ease the initial awkwardness and keep the conversation flowing.

To further enhance your social skills, create a social practice checklist. Include exercises like role-playing common scenarios, attending social skills workshops, and practicing active listening. Use this checklist to track your progress and celebrate your successes. Remember, improving social confidence takes time and practice, but with dedication and the right strategies, you can navigate social situations with greater ease and confidence.

As you work on building and maintaining healthy relationships, remember that social confidence is just one part of the puzzle. By understanding and addressing the unique challenges of ADHD, you can create meaningful and supportive connections. Next, we'll explore how to navigate career and professional life, offering tools and strategies to help you thrive in the workplace.

Chapter 6
Career & Professional Life

I was in a brainstorming session at work on a crisp autumn morning. As my colleagues discussed the upcoming manufacturing schedule, my mind buzzed with an array of ideas. I jotted down notes frantically, each concept building upon the last. By the end of the meeting, I had filled several pages with innovative approaches to increase efficiencies that I couldn't wait to share. This burst of creativity, a hallmark of my ADHD, often felt like my secret weapon. It allowed me to see connections others missed and develop unique and practical solutions.

Leveraging Creativity and Innovation in Your Career

Women with ADHD often possess a remarkable ability to think creatively and innovatively. This divergent thinking, which involves generating many ideas from a single starting point, can be a significant asset in the workplace. ADHD brains are wired to explore unconventional solutions, making you adept at finding novel solutions to complex problems. Research has shown that individuals with ADHD excel at tasks requiring conceptual expansion and overcoming knowledge constraints. For instance, you might invent creative uses for everyday objects or brainstorm new device features. This capacity to avoid fixation, or the tendency to stick to familiar ideas, allows for more original and groundbreaking creations.

To harness and showcase your creativity at work, seek roles that value and reward innovative thinking. Positions in marketing, design, product development, and creative writing are just a few examples where your unique skills can shine. Use brainstorming techniques like mind mapping to organize and expand your ideas. Mind mapping involves writing down a central concept and branching out with related thoughts and ideas. This visual representation can help you see the connections between ideas and develop more comprehensive solutions.

Collaboration with colleagues can also enhance your creative output. Working with others allows you to bounce ideas back and forth, building on each other's strengths and perspectives. For example, if you're working on a project that requires a fresh approach, gather a diverse team and facilitate a brainstorming session. Encourage everyone to share their ideas, no matter how unconventional they seem. This collaborative environment can lead to innovative breakthroughs that might not have been possible working alone.

To boost your creative thinking further, engage in daily creativity challenges. Set aside time each day to work on a creative task, whether writing, drawing, or brainstorming new ideas. These challenges keep your creative muscles sharp and can lead to unexpected insights. Journaling your ideas and reflections can also be beneficial. Write down any thoughts or concepts that come to mind, no matter how small or incomplete they may seem. Reviewing these entries regularly can help you identify patterns and develop your ideas further.

Engaging in creative hobbies outside of work can provide additional inspiration and improve your overall well-being. Activities like painting, crafting, or playing a musical instrument can stimulate your creative mind and give you a much-needed break from work-related stress. These hobbies offer a different way to express yourself and can often lead to new ideas to bring back to your professional life.

Now, let's look at Beth's success as an educator who used creative teaching methods to engage her students. Beth's ADHD allowed her to think on her feet and adapt her lessons to meet the diverse needs of her classroom. She incorporated interactive activities, multimedia presentations, and hands-on projects to make learning more engaging and effective. Beth's innovative approach improved her students' academic performance and made her a beloved and respected teacher.

Leveraging ADHD-related creativity can lead to remarkable success in various professional fields. By seeking roles that value creativity, using brainstorming techniques, collaborating with colleagues, and engaging in daily creative practices, you can harness your unique strengths and make a significant impact in your career.

Time Management at Work: Prioritizing Tasks and Deadlines

Imagine sitting at your desk with a pile of tasks in front of you. Emails are pinging, your phone buzzes with notifications, and deadlines loom. For many women with ADHD, managing time and prioritizing tasks can feel like an insurmountable challenge. Yet, effective time management is crucial for career success. It impacts productivity and performance, ensuring you meet your professional goals and reduce work-related stress. When you prioritize tasks efficiently, you can focus on what truly matters, accomplish more in less time, and create a more organized work environment. Effective time management leads to greater job satisfaction and control over your workload.

One practical tool to help prioritize tasks is the Eisenhower Matrix. This method, named after President Dwight D. Eisenhower, categorizes tasks based on urgency and importance. Divide tasks into four quadrants: urgent and important, important but not urgent, urgent but not important, and neither urgent nor important. Using this matrix, you can identify which tasks need immediate attention and which get scheduled for later or even delegated. This approach helps you focus on high-priority tasks, reducing the overwhelm from tackling everything simultaneously.

Another effective technique is the Pomodoro Technique. This technique involves working in short, focused intervals followed by brief breaks. Typically, you work for 25 minutes (one Pomodoro) and then take a 5-minute break. After completing four Pomodoros, you take a longer break of 15–30 minutes. This method helps maintain focus and prevents burnout by breaking your work into manageable chunks. It also encourages regular breaks, improving overall productivity and mental clarity. Allocate specific tasks throughout your day to your scheduled Pomodoros. For instance, dedicate the first Pomodoro of your workday to answering emails, then spend the next two on a high-priority project. Don't forget to take a short break between Pomodoros to create a structured routine and reduce the risk of getting sidetracked by less important tasks.

Setting clear, achievable goals and deadlines is essential for managing tasks effectively. It becomes easier to stay on track when you know the exact tasks you need to accomplish and establish a deadline. Refer to the task management techniques discussed in Chapter Three and implement the right strategies for you.

These techniques can prove themselves invaluable task management tools for professionals such as executive assistants, business managers, healthcare schedulers, or other professional women who struggle with managing their workloads. To implement these techniques, consider starting with a longer Pomodoro session at the beginning of your day and transitioning to a shorter Pomodoro session as the day progresses and decision fatigue sets in. Working in two 45-minute intervals first thing in the morning, then switching to 20-minute intervals after lunch may help you maintain concentration and avoid burnout. Set clear milestones for projects with measurable performance indicators. By breaking down tasks and setting specific deadlines, you can manage your workload more effectively and reduce stress.

Best Productivity Apps for ADHD

Productivity apps play a crucial role in managing ADHD. They offer a structured way to keep track of tasks, set reminders, and create schedules, which can significantly reduce the chaos that often accompanies ADHD. Technology acts as an external aid, helping you stay focused and organized. Apps designed with ADHD in mind can transform your approach to daily tasks, making them more manageable and less overwhelming. These tools help you remember important tasks and deadlines by providing visual and auditory cues. Choosing the right apps can make a world of difference, turning your smartphone into a powerful ally.

One standout app is Todoist, a task management tool that excels in organization. Todoist helps you create detailed task lists and categorize them into projects. You can set due dates, prioritize tasks, and even add subtasks. The app's clean interface makes it easy to see unfinished tasks, reducing cognitive load. Another excellent option is Trello, which uses a visual board and card system. Trello is perfect for managing and breaking projects into smaller, more manageable tasks. You can create boards for different projects, add lists for various stages, and move cards as tasks progress. This visual approach makes it easier to track progress and stay organized.

Focus@Will is a unique app designed to enhance concentration through music. It offers a selection of scientifically curated music channels to improve focus. You can customize the music to suit your preferences and needs, making it easier to stay on task. For those who enjoy a gamified approach to productivity, Habitica is an excellent choice. Habitica turns your tasks into a game, where completing tasks earns you rewards and progresses through levels. This playful approach can make task management more engaging and enjoyable.

Setting up these apps is straightforward. For Todoist, start by creating a project and adding tasks. You can set due dates, prioritize tasks, and break them down into subtasks. The app allows you to set recurring tasks, ensuring you never miss important deadlines. Trello involves creating boards for each project. Within each board, you can add lists to represent different project stages. Cards represent tasks that can be moved from one list to another as you progress. Customizing music channels in Focus@Will is simple. You can select from various genres, adjust the intensity, and set a timer for your focus sessions. Habitica requires setting up habits and tasks, which turn into game elements. Completing tasks earns you rewards, which are used to level up and unlock new features.

Integrating these productivity apps into your daily routine can transform how you manage tasks and projects. These tools provide the structure and support needed to navigate the challenges of ADHD. They offer a way to stay organized, reduce anxiety, and enhance focus, making your daily life more manageable and productive.

Advocating for Yourself in the Workplace

Imagine sitting in a meeting where your mind races with ideas but hesitates to speak up, fearing your thoughts might not be well-received. This hesitation can be habitual for women with ADHD, especially when the workplace doesn't fully understand or accommodate their needs. Self-advocacy becomes crucial here. Advocating for yourself ensures you can access the necessary resources and support to thrive. It reduces misunderstandings and conflicts, creating a smoother, more productive work environment. When your needs are met, job satisfaction and performance naturally improve, leading to a more fulfilling career.

One of the first steps in effective self-advocacy is preparation. Gather documentation and evidence that support your accommodation requests. This evidence could include a formal diagnosis, recommendations from healthcare providers, and examples of how specific accommodations have helped you in the past. Having this documentation ready can make your case more compelling when approaching HR or management.

Practicing assertive communication techniques is another crucial aspect of self-advocacy. Assertiveness involves expressing your needs and rights clearly and respectfully without aggression or passivity. For example, if you need a quieter workspace, you might say, "I've noticed that I work more efficiently in a quiet environment. Could we discuss possibly relocating my desk to a less noisy area?" This approach is direct yet polite, making it easier for others to understand and accommodate your needs.

Approaching HR or management with specific requests can feel daunting, but it's essential. Schedule a meeting to discuss your needs and bring your documentation. Be clear about what accommodations you require and explain how they will help you perform better in your role. For instance, if you're requesting a standing desk, demonstrate how the desk can enhance your productivity and reduce errors. The goal is to create a collaborative conversation where both parties work together to find solutions that benefit everyone.

Creating a supportive work environment goes beyond personal accommodations. Educating your colleagues about ADHD can foster understanding and reduce stigma. Share resources or hold informational sessions to explain how ADHD affects you and how they can support you. Building alliances with supportive coworkers can also make a significant difference. Having colleagues who understand your needs and advocate for you can create a more inclusive and supportive workplace culture. Participating in or creating employee resource groups focused on neurodiversity can provide additional support and resources. These groups can offer a platform for sharing experiences, discussing challenges, and finding collective solutions. This environment is also an excellent opportunity to secure a body double.

Additionally, evaluate when your productivity peaks. Do you perform your best work in the early morning, afternoon, and evening? Depending on your answer, a traditional 9-to-5 shift could be challenging. Prepare documentation from your healthcare provider and examples of your most productive periods. Schedule a meeting with your manager, explain your situation, and request altered work hours. The adjustment can lead to a significant improvement in your performance and job satisfaction.

Self-Employment and Entrepreneurship: Is It Right for You?

Imagine waking up each day with the freedom to set your schedule, pursue your passions, and work in an environment tailored to your needs; for women with ADHD, self-employment or entrepreneurship can offer these benefits and more. Flexibility and autonomy are among the most significant advantages. Being your own boss allows you to work during your most productive hours and create a routine that suits your unique rhythms. You can design a workspace that minimizes distractions and boosts focus, whether it's a quiet home office or a bustling coffee shop. This level of control can significantly reduce the stress and frustration often associated with traditional employment.

However, self-employment also presents unique challenges. Managing multiple roles and tasks can be overwhelming, especially when juggling marketing, accounting, client relations, and product development. The lack of external structure can make staying organized and prioritizing tasks difficult. Additionally, the financial instability and risks associated with entrepreneurship can be daunting. It's crucial to assess whether self-employment aligns with your strengths and lifestyle before taking the plunge.

To determine if self-employment is right for you, start with a self-assessment. Reflect on your strengths and weaknesses. Are you highly motivated and able to work independently? Can you manage time and tasks without external supervision? Consider your financial stability and risk tolerance. Entrepreneurship often involves initial financial uncertainty, so it's essential to have a safety net or alternative income stream.

Practical tools like self-assessment questionnaires can help you evaluate your suitability for self-employment. These questionnaires typically ask about your motivation, organizational skills, financial preparedness, and ability to handle stress. Be honest with yourself when answering these questions. If your strengths align with the demands of entrepreneurship, you may be well-suited for this path.

Once you've decided to pursue self-employment, developing a solid business plan is crucial. Outline your business goals, target market, competitive analysis, marketing strategy, and financial projections. Setting clear and achievable goals will help guide your efforts and measure your progress. Utilize productivity tools and apps to stay organized and manage your tasks efficiently. Apps like Trello, Asana, and QuickBooks can help you keep track of projects, deadlines, and finances.

Building a supportive network of mentors and peers is also essential. Surround yourself with individuals who understand the challenges of entrepreneurship and can offer guidance and encouragement. Join networking groups, attend industry events, and seek out online communities of like-minded entrepreneurs. A support system can provide valuable insights, resources, and emotional support.

Let's look at Monica, a coach who built a thriving practice. Monica's empathy and deep understanding of her clients' needs allowed her to offer personalized coaching services. She developed a business plan, set up a website, and used scheduling apps to manage her appointments. Monica also joined professional coaching associations and attended workshops to enhance her skills and network with other coaches. Her practice grew steadily, and she found great fulfillment in helping others achieve their goals.

Overall, self-employment and entrepreneurship can offer significant benefits for women with ADHD, including flexibility, autonomy, and the ability to create a tailored work environment. However, it is essential to assess your suitability for this path and prepare for its challenges. By developing a solid business plan, utilizing productivity tools, and building a supportive network, you can navigate the complexities of self-employment and thrive.

Chapter 7
Holistic Health & Well-Being

One sunny afternoon, I stood in my kitchen, staring at various colorful vegetables and fresh fish. It was a stark contrast to the processed, sugary snacks that used to fill my pantry. This transformation didn't happen overnight, but as I learned more about the connection between diet and ADHD, I realized that what I ate had a profound impact on my brain function and overall well-being. For many women with ADHD, dietary changes can be a game-changer, offering a natural way to manage symptoms and enhance daily life.

Nutrition and ADHD: Foods That Fuel Your Brain

Recognition in research and practice is increasing, validating the connection between diet and ADHD symptoms. Certain foods and nutrients are crucial to brain health, impacting cognitive function, focus, and energy levels. Omega-3 fatty acids in fatty fish like salmon, mackerel, and sardines are essential for brain health. These fats support neural communication and reduce inflammation, which can help improve ADHD symptoms like hyperactivity and inattention. Including sources of omega-3s in your diet can make a noticeable difference. Flaxseeds, chia seeds, and walnuts are excellent alternatives for plant-based options.

Conversely, sugar and processed foods can wreak havoc on your focus and energy levels. High-sugar diets are linked to increased inattention and impulsivity, making it harder to concentrate on tasks. Processed foods, often laden with unhealthy fats and additives, can cause energy crashes and exacerbate ADHD symptoms. A balanced diet, rich in whole foods, provides sustained energy and supports overall brain function. Ensuring that your meals include a good mix of proteins, fats, and carbohydrates helps maintain stable blood sugar levels, preventing the spikes and crashes that can disrupt focus.

Hydration is equally important. Dehydration can impair cognitive function, leading to difficulties in concentration and memory. Drinking enough water throughout the day is crucial for maintaining optimal brain performance. Herbal teas can also be a great way to stay hydrated while providing additional benefits, such as calming properties and antioxidants. Aim to drink at least eight glasses of water a day. Herbal teas, such as chamomile or peppermint, can be a soothing alternative to water and offer additional health benefits.

Creating a brain-healthy diet involves incorporating whole foods and minimizing processed items. Start by filling your plate with colorful fruits and vegetables rich in vitamins, minerals, and antioxidants. These nutrients support overall brain health and can help reduce inflammation. Including sources of omega-3 fatty acids is essential. Aim to have fatty fish like salmon or tuna at least twice weekly. If you're vegetarian or vegan, incorporate flaxseeds, chia seeds, or walnuts. These plant-based sources provide the necessary fats for brain function.

Balancing macronutrients is critical to sustained energy. Include a mix of proteins, fats, and carbohydrates in each meal. Proteins in foods like eggs, lean meats, and legumes help build and repair tissues and are essential for neurotransmitter production. Healthy fats, such as those from avocados, nuts, and olive oil, support brain health. Complex carbohydrates, like whole grains and vegetables, provide a steady energy source. Avoid simple carbohydrates found in sugary snacks and processed foods, as they can lead to energy crashes and increased ADHD symptoms.

Let's dive into specific dietary tips and meal ideas to help you manage ADHD symptoms. Breakfast is a crucial meal for brain health. Start your day with a brain-boosting option like a smoothie made with spinach, berries, flaxseeds, and a scoop of protein powder. This combination provides essential nutrients and sustained energy. For a quick and easy breakfast, try overnight oats with chia seeds, fresh fruit, and a drizzle of honey. This meal is rich in fiber, protein, and healthy fats, setting a positive tone for the day.

Snacks are an essential part of maintaining stable blood sugar levels and focus. Opt for nutrient-dense options like a handful of mixed nuts, apple slices with almond butter, or Greek yogurt with a sprinkle of flaxseeds. These snacks balance protein, fats, and carbohydrates, energizing you between meals.

For lunch and dinner, focus on nutrient-dense meals that support brain health. A grilled salmon salad with mixed greens, cherry tomatoes, cucumbers, and a vinaigrette made with olive oil and lemon juice is perfect. This meal provides omega-3 fatty acids, vitamins, and antioxidants. Another great option is a quinoa bowl with roasted vegetables, chickpeas, and a tahini dressing. Quinoa is a complete protein, and the vegetables offer a range of essential nutrients.

Meal prepping and planning can make sticking to a brain-healthy diet easier. Set aside time each week to plan your meals and snacks. Prepare ingredients in advance, such as chopping vegetables, cooking grains, and portioning snacks. This preparation ensures that you have healthy options readily available, reducing the temptation to reach for processed foods.

Nutritionist Dr. Sarah Brewer emphasizes the importance of a balanced diet for managing ADHD symptoms. "Eating a variety of whole foods, rich in essential nutrients, can support brain health and improve cognitive function. It's important to avoid processed foods and sugar, which can exacerbate symptoms."

By understanding the connection between diet and ADHD symptoms, you can make informed choices that support your brain health. Incorporating whole foods, balancing macronutrients, and ensuring adequate hydration can help manage ADHD symptoms and improve overall well-being. These dietary changes, practical tips, and meal ideas provide a foundation for a brain-healthy lifestyle.

Dietary Supplements for Managing ADHD Symptoms

Various dietary supplements are highly beneficial for combatting unwanted ADHD symptoms. These supplements can support cognitive function, emotional regulation, and overall health and are often used to manage symptoms like inattention, impulsivity, and mood swings. I will outline the benefits of each below.

> Always consult your doctor before starting a new dietary supplement regimen to ensure they will not interact with your other medications.

Additionally, it is wise to start by adding one supplement at a time. Wait at least two weeks before adding another supplement. This probationary period is crucial to identifying any potential side effects you may experience, as well as isolating the dietary supplement responsible. I experienced heart palpitations while taking Magnesium L-Theronate, so I immediately discontinued use.

Zinc

Benefits: Zinc plays a role in neurotransmitter activity, including dopamine regulation, essential for attention and focus. Zinc deficiency is linked to worsening ADHD symptoms.

Sources: Zinc gluconate, zinc picolinate.

Suggested Dosage: 30-40 mg per day.

Omega-3 Fatty Acids (Fish Oil)

Benefits: Omega-3s, particularly EPA and DHA, are crucial for brain health and cognitive function. Studies have shown that omega-3 supplementation can improve attention and focus and reduce hyperactivity in individuals with ADHD.

Sources: Fish oil, algae-based supplements for vegetarians/vegans.

Suggested Dosage: 1-3 grams per day (EPA/DHA combined).

Magnesium

Benefits: Magnesium supports neurotransmitter function and helps with relaxation, which can reduce hyperactivity and improve mood stability. It's also crucial for women's hormonal balance, which can impact ADHD symptoms.

Sources: Magnesium glycinate, citrate, L-Theronate.

Suggested Dosage: 200-400 mg per day.

B Vitamins (especially B6 and B12)

Benefits: B vitamins support brain function, particularly in producing neurotransmitters like dopamine and serotonin. Vitamin B6, in particular, may enhance the effectiveness of magnesium in managing ADHD symptoms.

Sources: B-complex supplements or individual B6/B12 supplements.

Suggested Dosage: Follow recommended daily allowance (e.g., 1.3 mg for B6, 2.4 mcg for B12), but therapeutic dosages for B6 can go higher (up to 50 mg under medical supervision).

Iron

Benefits: Low iron levels, especially ferritin (stored iron), have been linked to increased ADHD symptoms. Women, particularly those who menstruate, are at higher risk of iron deficiency.

Sources: Ferrous sulfate or ferrous bisglycinate.

Suggested Dosage: 10-30 mg daily (only if deficiency is confirmed).

L-theanine

Benefits: L-theanine, an amino acid found in tea, promotes relaxation without causing drowsiness. It can help improve focus and reduce anxiety, which is beneficial for managing ADHD symptoms.

Sources: L-theanine supplements, green tea.

Suggested Dosage: 200-400 mg per day.

Probiotics

Benefits: Gut health is increasingly linked to brain health through the gut-brain axis. Probiotics can improve digestion and mood, both of which can impact ADHD symptoms. Some studies suggest a healthy gut positively influences neurotransmitter balance.

Sources: Probiotic supplements with strains like Lactobacillus and Bifidobacterium.

Suggested Dosage: 10-20 billion CFU per day.

Ashwagandha

Benefits: Ashwagandha has been used traditionally in Ayurvedic Medicine as an adaptogen to manage stress, anxiety, and fatigue and promote overall well-being. Recent studies have also identified that Ashwagandha enhances synaptic plasticity and supports neurotransmitter balance (e.g., dopamine), which improves focus and reduces impulsivity.

Sources: Ashwagandha (Withania somnifera) supplements.

Suggested Dosage:

Standardized Extract (Root): Studies show that 600 mg per day (in two doses of 300 mg) effectively reduces stress and anxiety and improves cognitive function.

Root Powder: 1-2 teaspoons (approximately 3-6 grams) daily, mixed with water or food.

Vitamin D

Benefits: Vitamin D is vital for mood regulation and cognitive health. Low vitamin D levels are associated with increased ADHD symptoms. Women are at risk of deficiency, particularly in winter or with limited sun exposure.

Sources: Vitamin D3 supplements.

Suggested Dosage: 1,000-4,000 IU per day, depending on levels.

N-acetylcysteine (NAC)

Benefits: NAC is a precursor to glutathione, an important antioxidant. It may help reduce irritability and impulsivity, symptoms often present in ADHD, and it can also support mental clarity.

Sources: NAC supplements.

Suggested Dosage: 600-1,200 mg daily.

Ginkgo Biloba

Benefits: Ginkgo biloba may improve attention, memory, and mental clarity. Some studies suggest it may enhance blood flow to the brain and have neuroprotective effects, which can be beneficial for ADHD.

Sources: Ginkgo biloba supplements.

Suggested Dosage: 120-240 mg per day.

Rhodiola Rosea

Benefits: Another adaptogen in traditional Ayurvedic medicine, this plant helps the autoimmune system function better, reduces stress and fatigue, and can improve working memory. Rhodiola supports mental clarity and endurance, improving focus and cognitive stamina. It also promotes emotional regulation.

Sources: Rhodiola rosea supplements.

Suggested Dosage:

Standardized Extract: 200-400 mg daily (containing 3-5% rosavin and 1-2% salidroside).

A standard recommendation is 200 mg, taken once or twice a day. Depending on their tolerance and the severity of symptoms, some individuals may benefit from higher doses (up to 600 mg).

Dried Root or Powder: 1-2 grams daily.

American Ginseng

Benefits: Research suggests Ginseng improves memory, attention span, and processing speed. It reduces hyperactivity and impulsivity and modulates neurotransmitters to improve imbalances.

Sources: American ginseng (Panax quinquefolius) supplements.

Suggested Dosage:

Standardized Extract: Clinical studies on cognitive performance and ADHD have used doses between 200-400 mg daily.

Raw Root or Dried Powder: 1-2 grams per day.

This list of dietary supplements should not replace any existing medications your doctor prescribes. Please refer to this list as a valuable resource for identifying complementary treatments to alleviate heightened symptoms. Provide this list to your doctor and discuss which dietary supplements may be right for you.

> None of the dietary supplements listed in this book are a "cure" for ADHD.

Earthing for Managing ADHD Symptoms

Earthing (or grounding) refers to direct physical contact with the Earth's surface, typically by walking barefoot on natural surfaces like grass, soil, or sand. The Earth's surface is rich in negatively charged free electrons. When the body comes into direct contact with it, these electrons can flow into the body, potentially neutralizing free radicals and reducing inflammation. The physiological effects of earthing have been the subject of growing interest and study in recent years. Here's a more in-depth look at how earthing may affect the human body:

Reduction in Inflammation: One of the primary proposed mechanisms of earthing is the reduction of inflammation. When exposed to oxidative stress, free radicals can damage cells, leading to inflammation. Grounding may neutralize free radicals by supplying the body with negatively charged electrons from the Earth. This practice can help reduce oxidative stress and inflammation linked to numerous chronic diseases and aging (Chevalier et al., 2015).

Improvement in Sleep: Earthing affects sleep quality by regulating circadian rhythms and promoting deeper, more restorative sleep. Grounding helps synchronize the body's internal clock by normalizing cortisol levels, the hormone responsible for stress. Research has found that participants who slept while grounded reported better sleep and reduced stress (Ghaly & Teplitz, 2004). This regulation of sleep patterns can cascade positive effects on overall health, mood, and cognitive function.

Reduction in Pain and Muscle Soreness: Earthing is studied for its potential to alleviate pain and muscle soreness. This potential is partly because of its anti-inflammatory effects. In a study of athletes, those who practiced grounding after strenuous exercise experienced reduced muscle soreness and faster recovery (Brown et al., 2015). Chronic pain sufferers also reported reduced discomfort after grounding, likely due to decreased inflammation and improved circulation.

Cardiovascular Benefits: Earthing may positively influence the cardiovascular system by improving blood viscosity and flow. Blood clotting and high blood viscosity are risk factors for cardiovascular disease, including heart attacks and strokes. Research suggests that grounding can decrease blood viscosity and reduce the tendency of red blood cells to clump, thus enhancing circulation (Chevalier et al., 2012). Better blood flow can result in more efficient oxygen and nutrient delivery throughout the body.

Enhanced Immune Function: Earthing may support and improve immune function by reducing chronic inflammation and oxidative stress. Chronic inflammation correlates to numerous immune-related disorders. Grounding could assist the immune system by creating a more balanced physiological environment, which allows the body to focus on fighting infections or healing from injury (Oschman, 2007).

Reduction of Stress and Anxiety: Earthing has a calming effect on the nervous system. Studies indicate that grounding helps balance the autonomic nervous system (ANS), which regulates involuntary bodily functions such as heart rate, digestion, and respiratory rate. Many grounded participants show increased parasympathetic (rest-and-digest) activity and decreased sympathetic (fight-or-flight) activity, leading to reduced feelings of stress and anxiety (Chevalier, 2015). These changes can also improve heart rate variability (HRV), an indicator of cardiovascular health and stress resilience.

Regulation of Cortisol Levels: One of the most well-documented effects of grounding is its influence on cortisol, a hormone released in response to stress. Chronic stress leads to persistently high cortisol levels, which translates to a range of health problems, including sleep disturbances, weight gain, and immune suppression. Grounding can potentially normalize cortisol levels over long periods (Ghaly & Teplitz, 2004). Reducing cortisol can improve mood and mental health while also reducing stress.

Mood Enhancement and Mental Health Benefits: Earthing can have an overall stabilizing effect on mood. Individuals who engage in grounding often feel calmer, more centered, and less prone to emotional fluctuations. Grounding's improvements in stress, sleep, and inflammation may enhance mental health and well-being. For those with conditions such as anxiety or depression, grounding may offer a natural and holistic method to manage symptoms.

Electromagnetic Balance: Modern living exposes humans to significant amounts of electromagnetic radiation from devices like phones, computers, and Wi-Fi. Grounding may help reduce the body's electrical charge, which can accumulate over time due to this exposure. Some researchers argue that grounding restores the body's natural electrical balance, which may reduce the adverse effects of electromagnetic fields (EMFs) (Sokal & Sokal, 2011).

I discovered earthing when I watched *The Earthing Movie: The Remarkable Science of Grounding* by Rebecca and Josh Tickell on YouTube. They discussed how educators were using earthing as a coping strategy for students with learning disabilities and behavior disorders, specifically highlighting the benefits discovered for children with autism.

Earthing is the newest tool to my ADHD symptom management tool belt, but it is one of my favorites. I schedule as much natural grounding time as possible, meaning I want to be barefoot in the grass whenever possible. I am purchasing earthing mats for use in the house when it's raining, one for my office while I work, and earthing sheets for all my family members. The idea is to expose ourselves to as much grounding as possible. Sheets are a great option because they benefit us in the same way as passive income. You (hopefully) spend eight to nine hours sleeping in your bed every night. If you utilize grounding sheets, then you are recharging your body while you are already resting. Utilizing earthing sheets doesn't require changing your routine; you get an immediate return on your one-time investment.

This technique does not require purchasing fancy gadgets. It is as simple as walking outside, slipping your shoes off, and allowing yourself to connect to Earth for as long as possible. I only mention the gadgets as a means to the same end if you have the budget for them and need more time for a more natural approach.

Grounding is associated with a multitude of potential health benefits ranging from physical improvements such as pain relief and better sleep to emotional and mental well-being like reduced anxiety and stress. The reduction of inflammation, improved cardiovascular health, and enhanced immune function are particularly notable, offering a comprehensive way to support physical and mental health. While more research is needed, especially in larger and more diverse populations, the current evidence suggests that grounding may be a simple and accessible way to promote overall well-being.

Exercise as a Tool for Managing ADHD Symptoms

One evening, as I rolled out my yoga mat, I felt a familiar sense of anticipation. Yoga had become my go-to activity for managing my ADHD symptoms. Regular exercise has a profound impact on brain function, particularly for those with ADHD. Engaging in physical activity increases dopamine and serotonin levels, the neurotransmitters responsible for mood regulation and focus. These chemicals act like natural stimulants for the brain, helping to enhance attention and reduce hyperactivity. Over time, consistent exercise can also lead to long-term cognitive benefits, including improved memory and executive function.

Exercise is not just about physical fitness; it plays a crucial role in mood regulation and anxiety reduction. Physical activity triggers the release of endorphins, often called "feel-good" hormones, which can alleviate feelings of stress and anxiety. For women with ADHD, who frequently experience heightened emotional sensitivity, exercise provides a natural way to stabilize mood and improve overall well-being. The benefits extend beyond the immediate post-exercise glow. Regular physical activity contributes to better sleep, increased energy levels, and a more resilient mental state.

Incorporating exercise into a busy schedule can seem daunting, but setting realistic goals makes it achievable. Start by identifying activities you enjoy; you're more likely to stick with something fun. Whether it's dancing, swimming, or hiking, finding sustainable forms of exercise is key. Combining short, frequent workouts with longer sessions can offer flexibility. For instance, you might do a quick 10-minute workout in the morning and a longer session on the weekend. Using apps and tools to track your progress can also keep you motivated. Apps like MyFitnessPal or Fitbit can help you set goals, monitor your activity, and celebrate your achievements.

High-intensity interval training (HIIT) is an excellent, quick, effective workout option. HIIT involves alternating between short bursts of intense activity and brief rest periods. This exercise is time-efficient and highly effective for boosting cardiovascular health and metabolic rate. A simple HIIT routine might include 30 seconds of jumping jacks, followed by 30 seconds of rest, repeated for 10 minutes. Yoga and Pilates offer physical and mental benefits for those who prefer a more mindful approach. These practices enhance flexibility, strength, and balance while promoting relaxation and focus. Outdoor activities like hiking and cycling provide the added benefit of connecting with nature, which can be incredibly refreshing for the mind. Incorporating movement breaks throughout the day, such as a short walk during lunch or stretching between tasks, can also help maintain focus and energy levels.

As a busy mom, I often find myself overwhelmed by daily responsibilities. I struggled to find time for exercise until I discovered the power of short, quick workouts. Using 10-15 minute HIIT sessions three times a week has been the answer. These brief bursts of activity improve my fitness and boost my mood and focus, making it easier to manage my day. Attending a yoga class once a week also increases stress relief and mental clarity. My weekly yoga class is an escape, a sanctuary to unwind and center myself. The mindfulness aspect of yoga helps me manage my ADHD symptoms, providing a sense of peace and balance.

Outdoor activities can also offer significant benefits. I have found that walks through my local park provide a mental refreshment that no indoor activity can match. The combination of physical exertion and natural surroundings clears my mind and allows me to practice mindfulness and gratitude.

Exercise offers a powerful tool for managing ADHD symptoms, improving mood, and enhancing overall well-being. Regular physical activity impacts dopamine and serotonin levels, enhances focus, and reduces hyperactivity. Setting realistic exercise goals, finding enjoyable activities, and incorporating short and long workouts can make exercise a sustainable part of your routine.

Mindfulness Practices

Imagine sitting at your desk, trying to focus on a task, but your mind is racing in a hundred different directions. This scattered feeling is frequent for those with ADHD, but mindfulness can act as a powerful remedy. Mindfulness involves directing your attention to the present moment, which can significantly improve focus. For individuals with ADHD, staying present can help reduce the constant mental chatter and impulsive thoughts that often disrupt concentration. Mindfulness also plays a crucial role in reducing anxiety and stress. By focusing on the here and now, you can bypass the endless cycle of worry about past mistakes or future concerns. This anxiety reduction can lead to a calmer, more focused mind.

Additionally, mindfulness enhances self-awareness and emotional regulation. When you practice mindfulness, you become more attuned to your thoughts and feelings, fostering a deeper understanding of yourself. This heightened self-awareness can lead to greater self-compassion as you learn to treat yourself with kindness and understanding. The long-term effects of mindfulness and meditation on brain structure and function are well-documented. Research shows that consistent mindfulness practice can lead to structural changes in the brain, particularly in attention, emotion regulation, and self-control. These changes can enhance your ability to manage ADHD symptoms and improve overall cognitive function.

Various mindfulness practices can be particularly beneficial for the ADHD brain. Mindfulness-Based Stress Reduction (MBSR) is a structured program that combines mindfulness and yoga to reduce stress. Developed by Dr. Jon Kabat-Zinn, MBSR teaches you to be present and aware in each moment, helping to manage stress and improve overall well-being. Mindfulness-Based Cognitive Therapy (MBCT) is another effective method. MBCT combines traditional cognitive therapy with mindfulness practices to help break the cycle of negative thinking. This approach can be particularly helpful for those who struggle with emotional regulation and anxiety.

Incorporating mindfulness into your daily routine doesn't have to be complicated. Start by setting up a daily mindfulness practice. Dedicate a specific time each day, even if it's just five minutes, to practice mindfulness. Focus on the present moment while eating, walking, or washing dishes. Pay attention to the sights, sounds, and sensations around you. Practicing mindfulness during everyday activities can further enhance your ability to stay present. Whether washing dishes, walking, or eating, pay attention to the sensory experiences involved. Notice the textures, smells, and sounds, and bring your full attention to the activity.

Eckhart Tolle is a spiritual teacher and author whose work emphasizes the importance of mindfulness, inner peace, and living fully in the present moment. His most influential book, *The Power of Now*, outlines his teachings on how to transcend the mind's tendency to dwell on the past or project into the future and instead experience life fully in the present. The core message of his work is that true liberation and personal transformation come from disengaging from the ego-driven mind and achieving a state of conscious awareness.

Techniques for Practicing Mindfulness

Disidentifying from the Mind: Tolle stresses that people often mistake their thoughts and mind chatter for their identity. He encourages individuals to observe their thoughts without becoming attached to them, which helps create a state of "presence."

Body Awareness: A prominent technique in Tolle's approach is tuning into the body and its sensations. He suggests focusing on the body's internal energy field to anchor oneself in the present moment and reduce mental noise.

Conscious Breathing: Tolle advises using breathing exercises as a gateway to mindfulness. By focusing on the breath, individuals can bring their attention back to the present and disconnect from habitual thought patterns.

Observing the Pain-Body: Tolle introduces the concept of the "pain-body," an accumulation of past emotional pain that people carry with them. By bringing conscious awareness to this pain-body when it arises, one can begin to dissolve it.

Non-Judgmental Awareness: Tolle encourages a state of non-judgmental awareness in which one observes thoughts, feelings, and experiences without labeling them as good or bad. This acceptance fosters inner peace and prevents emotional reactivity.

Surrender to the Present Moment: Rather than resisting situations or trying to control outcomes, Tolle advocates for embracing the present moment as it is, even if it is uncomfortable. This surrender helps reduce suffering and opens one up to greater peace.

"What you resist not only persists but will grow in size." - Carl Jung

To practice mindful breathing, find a quiet place to sit. Close your eyes and take a deep breath through your nose, then slowly exhale through your mouth. Focus on the sensation of the air entering and leaving your body. Feel your neck stretch and collapse, just like an accordion. When your mind wanders, gently bring your attention back to your breath. Start with five minutes a day and gradually increase the time as you become more comfortable with the practice.

Incorporating mindfulness into your daily life can transform how you manage ADHD symptoms. By improving focus, reducing anxiety, and enhancing self-awareness, mindfulness offers a valuable tool for navigating the challenges of ADHD. Whether through mindful breathing, guided meditation, or MBCT, these practices can help you cultivate a calmer, more focused mind.

Meditation Practices

Dr. Joe Dispenza, a neuroscientist, chiropractor, and author known for his work on the intersection of neuroscience, epigenetics, and quantum physics, focuses on how thoughts and emotions can influence our biology and health. Dispenza's teachings often emphasize the power of meditation and visualization to facilitate personal transformation and healing. His popular books, such as *Breaking the Habit of Being Yourself* and *You Are the Placebo*, explore concepts of mindfulness, self-awareness, and the potential for individuals to create positive changes in their lives by changing their mindset.

Dr. Joe Dispenza's work delves into the concept that our thoughts and emotions can significantly impact our biology and genetics. He supports his ideas by integrating neuroscience, epigenetics, and quantum physics principles.

Neuroplasticity

Dispenza emphasizes the brain's ability to change and adapt. Through practices like meditation and visualization, individuals can rewire neural pathways, leading to new thought patterns and behaviors. This neuroplasticity suggests that consciously changing our thoughts can influence our mental and emotional states, ultimately affecting our physical health.

Epigenetics

He discusses how our environment and experiences can influence gene expression. Instead of being solely determined by our DNA, Dispenza proposes that our thoughts and feelings can activate or deactivate specific genes. We can enhance our well-being and resilience against disease by cultivating positive thoughts and emotions.

Mind-Body Connection

Dispenza underscores the link between the mind and body, illustrating how stress, anxiety, and negative thoughts can lead to physical ailments. Conversely, positive thinking and emotional states can promote healing and vitality.

Meditation and Visualization

Techniques that help individuals tap into their subconscious mind are central to his teachings. By engaging in deep meditation, practitioners can access altered states of consciousness that facilitate profound personal change, healing, and manifesting desired outcomes.

Quantum Physics

He incorporates ideas from quantum physics to suggest that our consciousness can influence the material world. This perspective encourages individuals to see themselves as active participants in shaping their reality rather than passive recipients of external circumstances.

Dispenza aims to empower individuals to harness their mental and emotional states for personal transformation, health improvement, and overall well-being through his workshops, lectures, and books.

Caren Magill, an ADHD Life Coach, posted her review of Dr. Joe's week-long retreat. She stated that it was more like a meditation rave due to the immersive nature of the retreat, cumulating in over 36 hours of meditation. Her top takeaways were:

1. **Our thoughts create our reality.** Where our attention goes, energy flows. Our energy creates our life. Speak kindly to yourself. Be the gatekeeper of your thoughts.

2. **Meditation and pure intent heal and magnetize.** It's true, and it's real. Emotionally and physically.

3. **The importance of energy centers and ADHD.** Imbalances in the third center - the digestive system. ADHD often has an impairment here, resulting physically in constipation, obesity, and a leaky gut. This chakra impairment appears mentally as overthinking, perfectionism, and lack of commitment or follow-through.

Caren stated that she would attend another retreat because the last two days of the retreat had a significant impact on her life. She did advise that it was only for some due to the intense meditation schedule. I have not personally attended one of Dr. Joe's retreats (YET). Still, I did purchase his guided meditation, *Tuning into New Potentials,* which was the catalyst for the publication of this book.

I felt like TV static was running rampant in my mind during my first or second meditation (before I knew anything about meditation or had finished reading *Becoming Supernatural*). As the meditation session progressed, the static spontaneously disappeared, and I had a completely clear and silent mind for the first time in 10 years. The focus and mental clarity I experienced were astounding to me. I immediately implemented daily meditation sessions during my lunch break to recharge and clear my exhausted and overtaxed brain. Creating a peaceful meditation space at home can enhance your practice. Choose a quiet, comfortable spot free from distractions. Add calming elements like cushions, candles, or soothing music.

One meditation technique is the body scan meditation, which promotes relaxation. Lie down or sit comfortably and slowly bring your attention to different body parts, starting from your toes and moving up to your head. Notice any sensations, tension, or discomfort, and allow yourself to relax. Loving-kindness meditation is another practice that fosters self-compassion. Sit quietly and repeat phrases like, "I am happy," "I am healthy," and "I am safe." This meditation can help cultivate a positive and compassionate attitude towards yourself.

Using guided meditation apps can provide structure and support. These apps offer a variety of guided sessions tailored to different needs and preferences. One app that stands out is Headspace, known for its user-friendly interface and variety of guided meditations. Headspace offers sessions tailored to different needs, whether you're looking to reduce anxiety, improve focus, or get better sleep. Setting up personalized meditation plans in Headspace is straightforward. Start by selecting your goal—be it stress reduction or enhanced focus. The app then guides you through a series of meditations designed to help you achieve that goal. You can choose the length of each session, making it easy to fit into your daily routine. The app also tracks your progress, offering gentle reminders to keep you on track.

Calm is another excellent option for those seeking relaxation and better sleep. The app features a wide range of sleep stories, narrated by soothing voices, that can help you drift off peacefully. Using Calm involves selecting a sleep story or relaxation technique from its extensive library. You can also set a timer to ensure you get the right amount of rest. The app's relaxation techniques, such as breathing exercises and progressive muscle relaxation, help reduce tension and promote a sense of calm. These features make Calm a versatile tool for managing stress and improving sleep quality.

Insight Timer offers a vast selection of meditation sessions, making it a go-to app for those who enjoy variety. You can explore meditation styles, from mindfulness to loving-kindness, and find what resonates. Setting up Insight Timer involves browsing its extensive library and selecting sessions that align with your needs. The app also features live events and community discussions, allowing you to connect with others on a similar journey. This sense of community can be incredibly supportive, offering additional motivation to maintain your mindfulness practice.

Breethe focuses on stress relief and emotional wellness, offering programs tailored to different aspects of life. The app features guided meditations, breathing exercises, and life coaching sessions. Accessing stress relief programs in Breethe is simple. You can choose from various programs designed to address specific issues, such as work stress or relationship challenges. The app guides you through each session, providing practical tools to manage stress and improve emotional well-being. Breethe's holistic approach makes it a comprehensive tool for enhancing mental health.

Meditation can offer profound benefits for managing ADHD symptoms and enhancing well-being. These practices improve attention, emotional regulation, and self-awareness. Various techniques, such as mindful breathing, body scan meditation, and loving-kindness meditation, can be tailored to your needs. Incorporating mindfulness into your daily routine can create a sense of calm and focus, helping you navigate the challenges of ADHD with greater ease and resilience.

Developing a Self-Care Routine That Works

Picture this: it's been a long day filled with meetings, errands, and countless demands. Your mind is racing, and your body feels drained. For women with ADHD, this scenario is all too familiar. Self-care isn't just a luxury; it's a necessity for managing ADHD symptoms and maintaining overall well-being.

Engaging in regular self-care practices helps reduce stress, which can exacerbate ADHD symptoms.

When you're less stressed, you're better able to regulate your emotions, making it easier to navigate daily challenges. Furthermore, self-care enhances focus and productivity by giving your brain the downtime it needs to recharge. Engaging in activities that bring joy and relaxation also boosts self-esteem and self-compassion, helping you see yourself more positively.

Creating a personalized self-care routine starts with identifying activities that genuinely bring you joy and relaxation. This act of self-love might include hobbies like painting, writing, gardening, or more structured activities like yoga or meditation. The key is to choose activities that resonate with you and provide a sense of fulfillment. Once you've identified these activities, schedule regular self-care time.

Treat these appointments with the same importance as work meetings or family obligations.

Consistency is crucial, so try to set aside time each day or week dedicated solely to self-care. Balancing self-care with other responsibilities can be challenging, but it's essential. Remember that taking care of yourself enables you to be more present and effective in other areas of your life. Feel free to adjust your routine as needed. Life is dynamic, and your self-care routine should be flexible enough to adapt to changing circumstances.

There are various self-care activities tailored to women with ADHD that you might find beneficial. Relaxation techniques like a warm bath can help soothe your mind and body. Adding aromatherapy with essential oils like lavender or eucalyptus can enhance the calming effect. Creative outlets such as journaling, painting, or crafting offer a way to express yourself and release pent-up emotions. These activities can be incredibly therapeutic, providing a break from the constant mental chatter. Physical self-care activities are equally important. Consider scheduling regular massages to alleviate muscle tension and promote relaxation. Stretching exercises can help improve flexibility and reduce physical discomfort. Social self-care involves spending quality time with loved ones. Whether it's a coffee date with a friend or a family game night, these interactions can provide emotional support and a sense of connection.

Ten years into my marriage and four children later, I have finally released the RIDICULOUS notion that self-care is selfish. My overwhelming life shoved me into a corner, and I felt like I was constantly fighting my way out, clawing, scratching, and pummeling many innocent bystanders along the way. When I noticed how severely out of balance my emotional regulation had become, I finally took a step back and evaluated what was going on in my life. I refused to be the mom remembered for her short temper or lack of energy for playing. This revelation lit a blazing fire under my tushy to get things figured out.

I found Dr. Joe's books and Eckhart's teachings posted on YouTube during this time. I started exploring yoga with my dear friend and decided that my children would survive my absence for two hours in the evening once a week. It was a feat of willpower to get out the door. The first night I went to yoga class, ALL of my children freaked out, even the eight-year-old… Being a mother, daughter, friend, sister, wife, and partner isn't easy. But we carry the divinity of creation. The power of life lies within us. Think about that and let that empowerment sink in. We cannot continue breathing life into others if we are empty. Make the time to refill the vessel you use every single day to bless others in your life. They will notice a difference and will encourage you to continue practicing self-love.

Developing a self-care routine that works for you is about finding a balance that fits your lifestyle and needs. It's not about perfection but about **making a commitment to prioritize yourself.** Self-care is a powerful tool for managing ADHD symptoms, enhancing emotional regulation, and improving overall well-being. By identifying activities that bring you joy, scheduling regular self-care time, and balancing it with other responsibilities, you can create a routine that supports your mental, emotional, and physical health.

In the next chapter, we'll explore strategies for navigating sensory overload, offering tools and techniques to help you create a more balanced and harmonious environment.

Share Your Story

Create Positive Change with Your Review

Tap into the Power of Generosity

> *"We make a living by what we get, but we make a life by what we give."*
>
> Winston Churchill

People who help others without expecting anything back often find greater happiness in life. So, let's make a difference together!

Would you help someone just like you—curious about living with ADHD but unsure where to start?

My mission is to make understanding and managing ADHD easy, fun, and empowering for everyone.

But I can't do it alone—I need your help.

Most people decide on a book based on reviews. So, I'm asking you to help someone just like you by leaving a review of *Women with ADHD: A Holistic, Practical and Actionable Approach to Embracing Your Uniquely Spectacular Brain.*

It costs nothing, takes less than a minute, but could change someone's ADHD journey. Your review could help...

...one more person feel seen and understood. ...one more woman discover helpful tips for managing her ADHD. ...one more person embrace their unique brain with confidence. ...one more woman realize that she is not alone. ...one more life to be completely transformed.

To make a difference, simply scan the QR code below and leave a review:

If making a difference brings you joy, you're exactly the kind of person I admire. My heartfelt thanks to you!

– Kayla Farr

Chapter 8
Parenting with ADHD

Every evening, as I try to cook dinner after work, all my children need me. My eldest daughter has a question about her homework. Our three-year-old wants to help me cook, and the twins demand to be held. The questions, crying, tugging on my clothes, clutching my leg, and, let's not forget, the food timer going off send my senses into chaos. The sound of boiling water, the sight of scattered toys, and the constant interruptions make it nearly impossible to focus. This moment of sensory overload and scattered attention highlights the unique challenges that come with parenting while having ADHD. These challenges can feel like a constant uphill battle for many of us.

Balancing Parenting Duties with ADHD

Parenting with ADHD presents a unique set of challenges that can complicate everyday tasks and responsibilities. One of the primary struggles is maintaining consistent routines and schedules. ADHD often makes it challenging to stick to a predictable routine, which children thrive on. The constant need to switch tasks can lead to missed appointments, forgotten school activities, and a general sense of disorganization. Managing sensory overload while caring for children adds another layer of complexity. The noise, clutter, and constant demands for attention can quickly become overwhelming, triggering a fight-or-flight response. Balancing attention between multiple children and tasks often feels like juggling, where one dropped ball can lead to a cascade of issues. Emotional dysregulation during stressful parenting moments can escalate conflicts and make it challenging to model calm behavior for your children.

To manage these challenges effectively, establishing consistent daily routines can be a game-changer. Consistency provides a structured environment that benefits both you and your children. Using visual schedules and checklists can help maintain these routines. Visual aids, such as colorful charts or magnetic boards, can make tasks and schedules more tangible and easier to follow. Delegating tasks and seeking help from partners or family members can alleviate some burdens. Sharing responsibilities ensures that everyone is safe and contributes to the household dynamics. It's essential to set realistic expectations and prioritize tasks. Not everything needs to be perfect; some days, getting through the basics is enough. A great resource is the book "Fair Play" by Eve Rodsky. Couple that with "The Fair Play Deck," a conversation starter/game meant to promote healthy communication between partners regarding household management, and you are equipped with the right tools to discuss sharing responsibilities with your partner.

Managing sensory overload and stress is crucial for maintaining a balanced home environment. Creating a sensory-friendly space at home can offer a retreat from the chaos. This space could include soft lighting, calming colors, and comfortable seating. Using noise-canceling headphones or earplugs during particularly overwhelming moments can help reduce auditory overload. Practicing deep breathing exercises can provide instant relief. Taking a few minutes to focus on your breath can calm your nervous system and help you regain composure. Remember to take short breaks to recharge. Even a five-minute break can make a significant difference in your stress levels. Step outside and bury your bare feet in the grass, stretch, or enjoy a quiet moment with a cup of tea. I often haul all the kids outside and let them burn off all that extra steam while I listen to the birds.

The biggest takeaway here is to understand that you will be overwhelmed. Your goal is to begin identifying those moments when it happens. Once you start doing that, everything else becomes more manageable. Try implementing an awareness strategy with your family. If sensory overload occurs, wear a funny hat or headband to draw attention to yourself. Explain to your children and partner that when you wear this hat, you need their help to create a sanctuary for sensory recovery. You will be amazed at how quickly children catch on to things like this.

You should also provide yourself abundant grace by setting realistic expectations and prioritizing tasks that significantly impact your daily life. **Every day will be challenging, so focus on completing the most critical tasks.** This mindset shift will also facilitate a different perspective on life. You might notice that the best task is concentrating exclusively on your children. Play with them for five minutes. Once they have conquered our attention, they often lose interest and move to the next best thing. Being present with our children is also a superb mindfulness practice. By surrendering to their request for attention, we acknowledge and validate their importance in our lives. Dinner will keep for five minutes.

On absolutely terrible days, I practice deep breathing exercises multiple times during overwhelming moments. I take a few minutes to step outside, close my eyes, and practice box breathing techniques until I regain calmness and composure. By understanding the unique challenges of parenting with ADHD and implementing practical strategies like establishing routines, using visual aids, delegating tasks, and managing sensory overload, you can create a more balanced and manageable home environment.

Teaching Your Children About ADHD

Talking to your children about ADHD fosters understanding and acceptance within your family. When you openly discuss ADHD, you reduce the stigma and misconceptions that often surround this condition. Children, like adults, develop biases and misunderstandings when accurate information isn't available. Educating them ensures they grow up with a clear and compassionate view of ADHD. This openness encourages empathy and support within the family, making it easier for everyone to understand and assist each other.

Explaining ADHD to children helps them understand their or a sibling's condition. When children know what ADHD is and how it affects behavior and attention, they are less likely to feel confused or frustrated by their own or sibling's actions. This understanding builds a foundation for open communication, where children feel comfortable asking questions and discussing their feelings. It allows them to express their concerns and challenges, fostering a supportive environment.

When explaining ADHD to younger children, it's critical to simplify complex concepts. Use relatable examples and stories that align with their everyday experiences. For instance, you might say, "Sometimes, your brain works like a race car, going very fast and making it hard to focus on one thing at a time." This analogy can help them grasp the idea without feeling overwhelmed. Providing educational books and videos about ADHD can also be beneficial. Resources like "My Brain Needs Glasses" by Annick Vincent or "All Dogs Have ADHD" by Kathy Hoopmann can make the topic more accessible and engaging.

Encouraging questions and discussions is another effective way to educate your children about ADHD. Create an open dialogue where they feel safe to ask anything they want to know. Answer their questions honestly and at an age-appropriate level. This ongoing conversation helps demystify ADHD and makes it a customary part of family life. You can foster a supportive family environment by teaching empathy and patience. Encourage your children to put themselves in each other's shoes and understand how ADHD might make specific tasks more challenging. Praise them when they show kindness and support toward their siblings. Consider holding family meetings where all family members can share their thoughts and feelings. Just remember to nurture an environment of learning, acceptance, support, and empathy.

Another critical aspect is encouraging siblings to support each other. Highlight the importance of teamwork and cooperation. For example, if one child struggles with organization, ask a sibling to help them tidy their room or keep track of their school supplies. Celebrating neurodiversity and unique strengths is also vital. Emphasize that everyone has different abilities and challenges, which makes each person unique. Involve your children in creating ADHD-friendly routines. Let them contribute ideas on how to make daily tasks easier and more enjoyable. This involvement gives them a sense of ownership and responsibility.

Effective Time Management for Moms with ADHD

Effectively managing time is paramount for moms with ADHD. It's not just about getting things done; it's about reducing the overwhelm and stress that naturally build up. When you have ADHD, every day can feel like a race against the clock, and without a clear plan, it's easy to feel like you're falling behind. Effective time management helps ensure quality time with your children, allowing you to be present and engaged rather than distracted and anxious. It also enables you to meet family and personal responsibilities, striking a balance that enhances your overall well-being and productivity.

One key strategy for managing your time is using digital calendars and reminders for scheduling. Digital tools can be lifesavers for moms with ADHD, providing a centralized place to keep track of appointments, activities, and deadlines. With a digital calendar, you can set reminders for important events and receive notifications to keep you on track. This tool is especially helpful for coordinating family schedules, as it keeps everyone informed and reduces misunderstandings. Additionally, implementing the "block scheduling" method can help you organize your day into manageable chunks of time. Block scheduling involves dividing your day into blocks dedicated to specific tasks or activities. For example, you might have a block for morning routines, one for work tasks, another for household chores, and a final block for family time. This method helps you stay focused and reduces the likelihood of getting sidetracked.

Prioritizing tasks with the "ABC" method is another effective strategy. This method involves categorizing tasks into three groups: A tasks must be done, B should be done, and C tasks are nice to do but optional. Focusing on the A tasks first ensures that the most critical responsibilities are addressed, reducing stress and making you feel more accomplished. Setting specific, achievable daily goals is also crucial. Rather than overwhelming yourself with a long to-do list, break your day into small, manageable goals. This approach makes tasks feel less daunting and provides a sense of achievement as you check off each item.

Several tools and resources can further aid in time management. Apps like Todoist and Trello are excellent for task management. Todoist allows you to create detailed to-do lists with deadlines and priorities, while Trello offers a visual way to manage projects using boards and cards. Family calendars and chore charts help keep everyone on the same page and ensure shared responsibilities. Timers and alarms are invaluable for structured time blocks, reminding you when to switch tasks. Journals for tracking daily progress can also be beneficial, helping you reflect on what you've accomplished and where you need to focus your efforts.

Using Digital Planners and Calendars Effectively

Managing your schedule and staying organized can be a challenge with ADHD, but digital planners and calendars can make a world of difference. These tools offer the convenience of accessing your plans across multiple devices, ensuring you always have your schedule at your fingertips. Visual and auditory reminders help you stay on track, reducing the likelihood of forgetting important tasks or appointments. The flexibility to adjust plans and functions as needed makes it easier to adapt to changes without feeling overwhelmed. Integration with other productivity tools means you can streamline your workflow, making daily routines more manageable.

Google Calendar stands out as a comprehensive scheduling tool. Its user-friendly interface allows you to set up events and reminders and invite others to meetings. You can color-code your events to visualize different aspects of your life, such as work, personal, and family. Google Calendar also syncs seamlessly with other Google services, providing a cohesive experience. Microsoft Outlook is another powerful tool, particularly for those who need integrated email and calendar management. It allows you to schedule events directly from your email and set reminders to ensure you get all the important deadlines and meetings. Notion offers an all-in-one planning and organization platform. Notion's flexibility lets you create custom templates for various needs, from daily to-do lists to complex project management. Any.do combines task and calendar synchronization, making it easy to manage your to-do lists alongside your schedule. Its simple interface and robust reminder system help you stay on top of your tasks.

Setting up events and reminders in Google Calendar is straightforward. Start by opening the app and clicking on the "Create" button. Enter the event details, set the time and date, and choose a color to categorize it. You can add reminders by selecting the "Add Notification" option, which allows you to set multiple reminders for each event. Integrating email tasks with calendar events in Outlook is just as simple. Click on an email, select the "More" option, and choose "Create Event." This action automatically populates the event details with information from the email, ensuring you capture all relevant details. Creating planning templates in Notion involves setting up a new page and choosing a template that fits your needs. You can customize it by adding text, checklists, tables, embedding other documents, and syncing tasks and calendars. Start with linking your calendar account. Once connected, you can view your tasks and events in a unified interface. Setting reminders is easy, and the app will notify you at the specified times.

The benefits of using digital planners and calendars for ADHD are immense. They offer a structured way to manage time, reduce stress, and increase productivity. By integrating these tools into your daily routine, you can navigate the challenges of ADHD more effectively. I swear by the Google Calendar app on my phone. Not only can I manage all our activities, but I can also use my phone to set reminders for myself too quickly.

"Hey, Google, remind me to print off the kids' shot records tonight at 8 pm."

Bam, I get a reminder to ensure a task is completed and my working memory is not overtaxed. I also previously mentioned our magnetic calendar on the fridge, which keeps everyone in our family in the loop for the month.

Most importantly, do what works best for you! **There is not a one-size-fits-all answer for moms with ADHD.** If becoming more organized feels too overwhelming, break your life into micro achievements. What is stressing you out the most? Laundry? OKAY! Only create a laundry schedule. Do this on paper or create a recurring event on your phone calendar to remind you to get it down. Once you have mastered this skill for one month, you will begin to feel confident and gain momentum for additional improvements in your life. Remember, you have been experiencing ADHD your entire life. You will not get everything fixed in one night, week, or month. Slowly add wins to your record, compounding your organization and time management improvements as you go. I know you can do this!

Creating a Supportive Home Environment

Creating a supportive home environment is crucial for both moms with ADHD and their families. A nurturing and organized space can significantly enhance emotional well-being and reduce stress. When your surroundings are in order, managing daily tasks and maintaining a sense of calm becomes easier. A supportive home encourages positive behavior and cooperation among family members. Conflicts are minimized when everyone clearly understands household expectations, and harmony reigns supreme. A stable home environment fosters a sense of stability and predictability, which is especially important for children. Knowing that certain routines and practices are consistent helps them feel secure and grounded. A supportive home also caters to the unique needs of each family member, ensuring that everyone feels valued and understood.

One practical approach to creating a supportive home environment is to establish clear and consistent routines. Routines provide a predictable structure that can help reduce anxiety and improve focus. For example, having a set bedtime routine can make evenings smoother and more relaxing. You might include reading a story, brushing your teeth, and conversing quietly before bed. Each step in the routine signals to your child that it's time to wind down, making the transition to sleep easier. Creating designated spaces for different activities can also make a significant difference. For instance, having a specific area for homework, another for play, and a separate space for relaxation helps everyone know what to expect in each part of the home. This organization can reduce clutter and make it easier to switch between activities without feeling overwhelmed.

Visual aids and reminders throughout the home can be particularly helpful for families with ADHD. Visual schedules, charts, and labels can serve as constant reminders of tasks and routines. For example, a morning routine chart in the bathroom can help children remember to brush their teeth, wash their faces, and get dressed. Posted chore charts decrease forgotten tasks. Open communication and family meetings foster a sense of unity and cooperation. Regular family meetings allow everyone to voice their concerns, share their successes, and plan for the week ahead. These meetings help resolve conflicts and ensure that everyone feels heard and valued.

Organizing and decluttering the home is another essential aspect of creating a supportive environment. Implementing a "one in, one out" rule for belongings can help keep clutter at bay. Whenever you bring a new item into the home, find an old item to donate or discard. This practice prevents accumulation and ensures that everything has its place. Using storage solutions like bins and labels can also make a significant difference. Clear bins with labels can help everyone know where things belong, making it easier to maintain order. Regularly decluttering and donating unused items can free up space and make the home more open and inviting. Involving the whole family in cleaning and organizing tasks can make these chores collaborative. Assign age-appropriate tasks to each family member and work together to tidy the home.

Creating a supportive home environment involves establishing routines, organizing spaces, using visual aids, and fostering open communication. These strategies can enhance emotional well-being, encourage positive behavior, and provide a stable foundation for your family.

Chapter 9
Financial Management

One Saturday morning, I sat at my kitchen table, bills scattered around me, a cup of cold coffee by my side. Seeing the unpaid bills and the confusion over where my money had gone that month filled me with dread. My ADHD brain had once again turned my finances into a chaotic mess. If you've ever felt this way, you're not alone. Managing money can feel overwhelming, particularly when ADHD makes organization and tracking details a constant struggle. Yet, gaining control over your finances is possible and incredibly empowering.

Budgeting Hacks for the ADHD Mind

Budgeting is crucial for financial stability, especially for those of us with ADHD. It provides a clear roadmap of where your money is going and helps you make informed decisions. Losing track of expenses is too easy without a budget, leading to financial stress. Regularly tracking income and expenses allows you to see patterns in your spending, helping you identify areas where you can cut back. This proactive approach to financial management can significantly reduce anxiety and provide a sense of control over your finances.

Budgeting also plays a vital role in achieving financial goals. Whether you want to save for a vacation, pay off debt, or build an emergency fund, having a clear financial plan is essential. A budget helps you allocate funds towards these goals, ensuring steady progress. Beyond goal-setting, a well-maintained budget can help you avoid unnecessary debt and live within your means. I cannot overstate the peace of mind derived from understanding your financial situation is under control.

For those of us with ADHD, traditional budgeting methods can feel too rigid or complicated. Fortunately, several ADHD-friendly budgeting techniques cater to our unique needs. One popular method is the "50/30/20" rule, which divides your income into three categories: 50% for needs, 30% for wants, and 20% for savings. This straightforward approach simplifies decision-making and ensures a balanced allocation of funds. Another effective technique is the envelope system, where you allocate cash into envelopes for different spending categories. This visual and tactile method helps you stay within budget and avoid overspending. To set up a 50/30/20 budget, calculate your monthly take-home pay. Allocate 50% of this amount to essential expenses like rent, groceries, and utilities. Next, designate 30% for discretionary spending, such as dining out, entertainment, and hobbies. Finally, allocate 20% to savings or debt repayment. Track your spending in each category to ensure you stay within these limits.

Digital budgeting tools and apps can also be a game-changer. Apps like YNAB (You Need A Budget) offer intuitive interfaces and real-time tracking, making it easier to monitor your finances. Zero-based budgeting is another method that works well for ADHD brains. This approach involves assigning every dollar a job, ensuring that your income and expenses balance out to zero. It provides a detailed view of your financial situation and helps prevent overspending.

If you prefer the envelope system, identify your spending categories, such as groceries, entertainment, and transportation. Allocate a specific amount of cash to each envelope based on your budget. Use only the cash in each envelope for its designated purpose. Once the money is gone, avoid spending in that category until the next budgeting period. This method provides a clear visual representation of your spending and helps curb impulsive purchases. There is also a digital version of the cash envelope method called Qube Money. This digital method can significantly limit the reckless stress spending ADHD women can do when their impulse control is too low. To summarize, you can only spend if the expense is planned and allocated. Can you think of a better way to stop impulsivity in its tracks?

If all else fails, head over to the blog of Rosemarie Groner, *The Busy Budgeter*. She has countless resources available for managing money, especially when you are overwhelmed!

Automating Finances: Simplifying Bill Payments and Savings

When managing finances feels overwhelming, automating your bills and savings can be a game-changer. For those of us with ADHD, the benefits are significant. Automating bill payments reduces the risk of missed payments and late fees, which can add up quickly and damage your credit score. Establishing automatic bill payments ensures bills get paid on time without the stress of remembering due dates. This consistency simplifies monthly financial tasks, freeing up mental space for other priorities.

To set up automatic bill payments, start with your online banking platform. Most banks offer this service for free. Log into your account, navigate the bill payment section, and add regular bills. Set the payment frequency and amount, ensuring it aligns with your billing cycles. Some apps can also help you track and manage these automatic payments. Using apps like Mint or Prism can provide a consolidated view of your finances, making it easier to monitor your cash flow. Ensure that you have sufficient funds in your account to cover these payments to avoid overdraft fees. Regularly check your account to ensure that payments are processed correctly.

Automating savings contributions is another effective strategy. Regular savings can often fall by the wayside when juggling multiple responsibilities. By setting up automatic transfers to a savings account, you ensure consistent contributions without having to think about it. Over time, these small, regular deposits can grow into a substantial savings cushion. This approach helps you build wealth and enhances your overall financial organization, making it easier to manage your money effectively.

Automating savings contributions is equally straightforward. Set up an automatic transfer from your checking account to your savings account. Choose a frequency that works for you, whether weekly, bi-weekly, or monthly. Round-up apps like Acorns can also help. These apps round up your everyday purchases to the nearest dollar and invest the spare change. This method is a painless way to save and invest without significant effort.

Additionally, automating contributions to retirement accounts like a 401(k) or IRA can ensure you consistently save for your future. Set specific savings goals and timelines to keep yourself motivated and on track. Using round-up apps can also make a significant difference. Using an app like Acorns makes saving effortless. Each purchase contributes a small amount to your savings, accumulating over time. The convenience of this method suites most ADHD brains perfectly, as it requires minimal effort and thought.

Also, consider adding your recurring bills to a digital calendar (I'm referring to you, my precious Google Calendar). This app has saved me on more than one occasion by having a place to quickly reference what and how much is coming out of our bank account. Simply add the bills as recurring events in your calendar and put the bill amount in the description. For example, you could put a monthly recurring event for your water bill and title it "Water Bill $40". It is also beneficial to color-coordinate recurring events. All my bills are red. All our paydays are green (helpful if you and your partner have different pay periods). Personal events are purple (think birthdays), and upcoming appointments are yellow. This is one method that I have found to help my brain process information more quickly.

By incorporating these automation strategies, you can simplify your financial management and reduce the stress of handling money. The consistency and reliability of automated systems can provide a sense of control and stability, making it easier to focus on other aspects of your life.

Managing Impulse Spending

Impulse spending can feel like an unshakable habit, especially for those of us with ADHD. The link between ADHD and impulsivity is well-documented. Our brains crave dopamine, and buying something new provides that quick hit of pleasure. This experience can lead to emotional triggers for impulse spending, such as stress, boredom, or excitement. The financial consequences of these spur-of-the-moment purchases can be severe, leaving us with dwindling bank accounts and rising credit card debt. Over time, these habits can erode financial stability, making it crucial to address and manage impulse spending effectively.

One practical strategy to curb impulse spending is implementing a "cooling-off" period before purchasing. When you feel the urge to buy something, wait 24 hours. This practice gives you time to evaluate whether you truly need the item or it's just a fleeting desire. Another effective method is using cash for discretionary spending. By carrying only a specific amount of cash, you limit yourself to what's in your wallet, reducing the temptation to overspend.

Similarly, using the digital cash envelope system, Qube Money limits your thoughtless spending because you must approve the amount. Setting clear spending limits and sticking to them can also help. Define a budget for non-essential items and make it a rule to stay within this amount. Avoiding online shopping temptations is equally critical. To minimize temptation, delete saved payment information from frequently visited online stores and unsubscribe from retail emails.

To build better spending habits, consider keeping a spending diary. Track every purchase you make, no matter how small. This exercise helps you become more aware of your spending patterns and identify moments of impulsivity. Reflecting on emotional triggers for impulse buying can provide valuable insights. Ask yourself what emotions led to the purchase and how you felt afterward. Creating and following a monthly spending plan can give structure and help you stay on track.

Creating a monthly spending plan can help you build better spending habits. List all your fixed and variable expenses and set a limit for discretionary spending. Review this plan regularly to ensure you're sticking to it. Reflecting on emotional triggers can also be insightful. Keep a journal where you note what you felt before an impulse buy and how you felt afterward. This reflection can help you understand the emotional patterns driving your spending and develop strategies to manage them.

Another strategy is to practice mindful shopping. Before making a purchase, take a moment to pause and ask yourself a few questions: Do I need this item? Will it add value to my life? Can I afford it within my budget? Is this a want or a need? Does this align with my financial goals? This pause can disrupt the automatic impulse to buy and provide a moment of clarity.

While we are on mindfulness, consider your relationship and mindset about money. Do you carry limiting beliefs that you aren't good with money? Do you believe that only evil people have money? Morgan Housel's "The Psychology of Money" discusses how no one is crazy regarding how they spend money because everyone can justify their reasoning based on their upbringing, challenges, opportunities, culture, and personal beliefs. For example, spending 10,000 dollars on a hotel room is unwise to me, but a member of the elite wouldn't balk a moment at such a routine expense. Also, many beliefs about money are so subconscious that we don't even realize them. I recommend taking a magnifying glass to your beliefs to see if they serve or limit you. If you want to dig even deeper, check out Rhonda Byrne's film *The Secret* on YouTube. I listen to it multiple times daily to get encouraged and remind myself that I shape my destiny, including my relationship with money.

By understanding the challenges of impulse spending and implementing these practical strategies, you can take control of your finances and reduce the stress associated with impulsive purchases. Combining reflective exercises, mindful shopping techniques, limiting belief evaluation, and structured spending plans can help you develop healthier financial habits and achieve greater financial stability.

Financial Planning for the Future

Long-term financial planning is a cornerstone of achieving future goals and ensuring financial security, especially for those of us with ADHD. Setting clear financial goals helps create a roadmap for where you want to go, providing direction and purpose. Without these goals, it's easy to feel adrift, unsure whether you're progressing. A long-term financial plan reduces financial uncertainty by laying out a clear path to follow, allowing you to anticipate and prepare for future expenses. This forward-thinking approach is crucial for overall financial well-being, enabling you to make informed decisions that align with your long-term objectives.

Creating and working towards financial goals requires actionable strategies. One effective method is setting SMART goals—Specific, Measurable, Achievable, Relevant, and Time-bound. For instance, instead of a vague goal like "save more money," a SMART goal would be "save $5,000 for an emergency fund within one year." This specificity provides a clear target to aim for, making it easier to measure progress. Breaking down these long-term goals into smaller, manageable steps is essential. If your goal is to save for a down payment on a house, identify monthly savings targets contributing to this larger objective. Regularly reviewing and adjusting your financial goals ensures they remain relevant and achievable. Celebrate milestones and progress along the way to stay motivated and acknowledge your efforts.

Retirement planning is a critical component of long-term financial planning. The first step is understanding different retirement accounts, such as 401(k) plans and IRAs (Individual Retirement Accounts. A 401(k) plan is typically employer-sponsored, allowing you to contribute pre-tax income, while an IRA is an individual account with various tax benefits. Calculating your retirement savings needs involves estimating future expenses and considering factors like inflation and life expectancy. Online retirement calculators can provide a ballpark figure. Automate contributions to your retirement accounts to ensure consistent savings. Seeking professional financial advice can also be invaluable. A financial advisor can help tailor a retirement plan to your needs and goals.

To apply these strategies, start by setting your own SMART financial goals. Write them down and break them into smaller steps. Use tools like online calculators to estimate retirement savings needs and automate contributions to ensure consistency. Regularly review your goals and adjust them as needed. Celebrate your progress to stay motivated and recognize your achievements.

By focusing on long-term financial planning, you can create a clear path towards achieving your future goals and ensuring financial security. Setting and working towards SMART financial goals, breaking them down into manageable steps, and regularly reviewing your progress will help you stay on track. Understanding and planning for retirement ensures you prepare for the future. These strategies reduce financial uncertainty and contribute to overall financial well-being, providing peace of mind and control over your financial future. The next chapter will explore strategies for navigating sensory overload and offer tools and techniques for creating a more balanced and harmonious environment.

Chapter 10
Navigating Sensory Overload

One summer afternoon, I was at a bustling outdoor market filled with vibrant colors, tantalizing smells, and a cacophony of sounds. The energy was palpable, yet within minutes, I felt an overwhelming urge to escape. My heart raced, my head pounded, and the once enticing atmosphere became a suffocating maze. This internal attack was a classic instance of sensory overload, a challenge many women with ADHD face daily. Sensory overload can turn ordinary experiences into overwhelming ordeals, making understanding and managing our sensory triggers crucial.

Identifying Your Sensory Triggers

Sensory overload occurs when your brain is overwhelmed by sensory input, leading to an overreaction or shutdown. For individuals with ADHD, heightened sensory sensitivity is common, causing everyday stimuli to feel intense and unmanageable. This heightened sensitivity can manifest in various ways, including trouble focusing, restlessness, and extreme irritability. Imagine being in a brightly lit room with loud noises and strong smells and feeling your senses attacked from all directions. This symptom can significantly impact daily functioning and mental well-being, often leading to anxiety and avoidance of specific places or situations.

Identifying your sensory triggers is the first step in managing sensory overload. One effective method is to keep a sensory journal. This practice involves writing down your reactions to different sensory inputs throughout the day. Track your actions, feelings, and physical or emotional responses. Over time, patterns will emerge, helping you pinpoint specific triggers. Reflecting on past experiences of overwhelm can also provide insights. Think about situations where you felt particularly overstimulated. What were the common elements? Was it the noise level, the lighting, or perhaps certain smells?

Using sensory checklists can be another helpful tool. These checklists often include common triggers such as bright lights, loud noises, and specific textures. You can systematically identify which stimuli affect you the most by going through a checklist. Additionally, seeking input from close friends or family members can offer valuable perspectives. They might notice patterns or triggers that you have overlooked.

Increasing sensory awareness is essential for better management of sensory overload. Sensory inventory worksheets can guide you in documenting your sensory preferences and sensitivities. These worksheets help you categorize different sensory inputs, making it easier to identify problematic ones. Mindfulness exercises focused on sensory experiences can also enhance awareness. Spend a few minutes daily paying attention to one sense at a time. For example, close your eyes and focus on sounds around you, noting their pitch, volume, and rhythm. This practice can help you become more attuned to your sensory environment.

Reflective journaling on sensory reactions is another effective exercise. After a particularly overwhelming experience, take some time to write about what happened. Describe the sensory inputs and your physical and emotional responses. This reflection can deepen your understanding of your triggers and help you develop strategies to manage them. You can take proactive steps to manage sensory overload by understanding and identifying your sensory triggers. Each sensory journey is unique; what works for one person might not work for another. The key is to be patient and persistent in finding the strategies that best suit your needs. You can create a more balanced and harmonious life by becoming more attuned to your sensory environment.

Creating a Sensory-Friendly Home

Creating a sensory-friendly home can significantly enhance your comfort and relaxation. For women with ADHD, sensory overload often turns the home into a place of stress rather than solace. Imagine entering a sanctuary where every element soothes and calms. This type of environment can dramatically reduce sensory-induced stress and anxiety, making it easier to unwind after a long day. When your home minimizes sensory triggers, it becomes a haven where you can recharge, supporting your mental and physical well-being.

A sensory-friendly home also supports focus and productivity. Bright lights, clutter, and noise can distract you, making it hard to concentrate on tasks or projects. Designing spaces that limit these distractions creates an environment conducive to clear thinking and efficient work. Additionally, a well-designed, sensory-friendly home promotes better sleep and rest. Soft lighting, calming colors, and comfortable textures signal to your brain that it's time to wind down, improving your sleep quality and overall restfulness.

To begin transforming your home, start with lighting. Use soft lighting and natural light sources whenever possible. Harsh, fluorescent lights can be overwhelming, while softer, warmer lights create a calming atmosphere. Natural light boosts mood and energy levels, so open your curtains during the day to let the sunshine in. Incorporating calming colors and textures also plays a crucial role. Shades of blue, green, and lavender are known for calming effects. Choose these colors for your walls, furniture, and decor. Soft, plush fabrics for cushions and throws can add an extra layer of comfort.

Reducing clutter and organizing spaces can significantly lower sensory stress. A cluttered environment can make it difficult to focus and relax. Use storage solutions like bins, shelves, and cabinets to keep your belongings organized and out of sight. Designate specific areas for different activities to maintain order. For example, have a dedicated space for work, another for relaxation, and another for hobbies. Soundproofing materials and white noise machines can help manage auditory sensitivities. If noise is a significant trigger, consider adding rugs, curtains, and soundproof panels to absorb sound. White noise machines can mask disruptive background noises, helping you concentrate or sleep better.

Different areas of the home require specific strategies to be sensory-friendly. In the bedroom, focus on creating a calming retreat. Use blackout curtains to block out light and ensure the room is cool and dark. Soft, breathable bedding can enhance comfort. A weighted blanket can provide a sense of security and help with relaxation. For the living room, choose furniture that is both comfortable and supportive. Arrange the furniture to create cozy nooks for reading or relaxing. Consider a neutral color palette with pops of calming colors. Keep the space tidy and clutter-free to promote relaxation.

Setting up a quiet workspace is essential for productivity. Choose a location away from high-traffic areas and minimize visual distractions. A comfortable chair and a desk with ample space can make working more enjoyable. Use organizers to keep your work materials in order. Soundproofing your workspace can further enhance focus. In the kitchen, organize your supplies to minimize clutter and make everything easy to find. Use clear containers for dry goods and label them for quick identification. Soft lighting and calming colors can make the kitchen a more pleasant space to cook and eat.

Creating a sensory-friendly home involves thoughtful adjustments to lighting, colors, textures, and organization. By tailoring your home to your sensory needs, you can reduce stress, enhance relaxation, and support better focus and sleep. These changes can transform your home into a true sanctuary, providing a comforting and supportive environment for you to thrive.

Coping Strategies for Sensory Overload in Public

Navigating public spaces can be a daunting task for those of us with ADHD. The unpredictability of sensory stimuli can be overwhelming, from the cacophony of sounds to the barrage of visual distractions. Imagine walking through a busy mall with bright lights, loud music, and crowds. Each sensory input feels like an attack, making it difficult to focus on anything else. The lack of quiet or calming spaces in public environments only exacerbates the situation, leading to emotional and physical exhaustion. This constant state of heightened alertness can drain your energy, making it crucial to develop strategies for managing sensory overload in these settings.

Planning and preparing for sensory triggers can make a significant difference. Before heading out, take a moment to think about the environment you'll be entering. Identify potential triggers and plan accordingly. For example, if you're going to a noisy restaurant, consider visiting during off-peak hours when it's less crowded. Carrying sensory tools like noise-canceling headphones can help block out overwhelming sounds. These headphones can be a lifesaver in noisy environments, allowing you to focus and stay calm. Identifying and utilizing quiet spaces can also provide relief. Many public places have designated quiet areas, such as libraries or coffee shops with cozy corners. Knowing where these spaces are can give you a place to retreat when things become too overwhelming.

Psychological grounding techniques and mindfulness practices can also be effective. Psychological grounding techniques involve focusing on the present moment and using your senses to anchor yourself. One simple technique is the 5-4-3-2-1 exercise: identify five things you can see, four things you can touch, three things you can hear, two things you can smell, and one thing you can taste. This exercise can help you regain control and calm your mind. Mindfulness practices, such as deep breathing exercises or guided meditation, can reduce anxiety and help you stay centered in chaotic environments.

Different public settings present unique challenges and require tailored strategies. In crowded places like malls and airports, try to avoid peak times when they are most crowded. Use the layout to your advantage by staying near the edges of crowds and avoiding central, congested areas. If you need a break, find a quiet corner or a less busy store to collect your thoughts. Creating a sensory-friendly workspace can help manage sensory overload at work or school. Use desk dividers or cubicle walls to minimize visual distractions and noise-canceling headphones to block background noise. Take regular breaks in a quiet area to recharge.

Social events can be particularly challenging due to sensory stimuli and social expectations. Arriving early to these events can help you find a comfortable spot before the crowd arrives. Communicate your needs to friends or hosts so they understand if you need to step outside or take a break. During travel, sensory overload can be intense due to the constant changes in environment and routine. Pack a sensory toolkit with noise-canceling headphones, weighted blankets, or fidget toys. Use grounding techniques during flight takeoffs and landings to stay calm.

Navigating sensory overload in public settings can be challenging, but with the right strategies, you can manage your sensory sensitivities effectively. By planning and preparing for sensory triggers, using sensory tools, and practicing grounding techniques, you can reduce the impact of sensory overload and navigate public environments with greater ease.

The Role of Sensory Tools and Gadgets

Amid a particularly chaotic day, I found solace in the simple act of squeezing a stress ball. The repetitive motion and tactile sensation provided an instant sense of calm. For many women with ADHD, sensory tools and gadgets can be incredibly effective in managing sensory sensitivities. These tools range from noise-canceling headphones and earplugs to fidget toys and weighted blankets. Each serves a unique purpose, helping to mitigate the overwhelming sensory input that often accompanies ADHD.

Noise-canceling headphones and earplugs are invaluable for those who are sensitive to sound. They create a barrier against auditory distractions, allowing you to focus and remain calm in noisy environments. Fidget toys and stress balls channel nervous energy and provide a tactile distraction that can be incredibly soothing. Weighted blankets and vests apply gentle pressure, creating a sense of security and relaxation, like a comforting hug. Aromatherapy diffusers and calming scents, such as lavender, eucalyptus, or chamomile, can also play a significant role in creating a tranquil atmosphere, helping to ease anxiety and improve focus.

Assessing your personal sensory needs and preferences is crucial when selecting sensory tools. What works for one person might not work for another. Take the time to try out different tools to find what resonates with you. For instance, noise-canceling headphones are perfect for work, but a weighted blanket is more beneficial during relaxation time at home. Integrating these tools into your daily routines and environments can make a significant difference. Keep your fidget toys within reach at your desk, and use an aromatherapy diffuser during your evening wind-down routine. Maintaining and caring for your sensory gadgets is also important. Regularly clean and check them to ensure they remain effective and in good condition.

Creating a personalized sensory toolkit can be a game-changer. Start by selecting essential items tailored to your specific needs. The kit might include a pair of noise-canceling headphones, a few fidget toys, a small bottle of calming essential oil, and a weighted blanket. Consider portable sensory tools for on-the-go use. A small fidget toy or a stress ball can easily fit into your purse, providing instant relief whenever needed. Storing and organizing your sensory toolkit in an accessible place ensures you can quickly grab what you need. Regularly update your toolkit based on changing needs or discoveries. Remember, your free sensory regulator is available 24 hours a day, Mother Earth! If you are in a social situation where you feel uncomfortable removing your shoes, simply sit on the ground and place your hands on the earth to achieve the same grounding effect.

Using sensory tools and gadgets can profoundly impact your ability to manage sensory sensitivities. You can create a more balanced and harmonious life by carefully selecting, integrating, and maintaining these tools. Creating a sensory-friendly environment at home, identifying personal sensory triggers, and utilizing sensory tools all contribute to managing ADHD effectively. Each strategy provides a unique way to navigate the challenges of sensory overload, helping you find peace and focus in your daily life.

Chapter 11

Embracing Your ADHD Superpowers

One evening, I was sitting at the dining table, surrounded by craft supplies, scraps of paper, and a half-finished scrapbook. The world outside seemed to blur as I snipped away at family photos, pairing each with the cutest frames and accessories. I wasn't just scrapbooking; I was experiencing an escape, a moment of pure creative flow where my ADHD felt like a gift rather than a burden. You might recognize this feeling if you've ever lost yourself in a creative project. It's the magic of ADHD, a unique ability to see the world differently, to think outside the box, and to create in ways others might not.

The Creative Power of ADHD

ADHD often comes with a unique brand of creativity. This spectacular gift isn't just anecdotal; research supports that individuals with ADHD frequently excel in creative thinking and problem-solving. The link between ADHD and creativity lies in what psychologists call "divergent thinking." While others might follow a linear path to solve problems, your ADHD brain can make connections between seemingly unrelated ideas, leading to innovative and original solutions. This ability to think outside the box is a hallmark of ADHD and can be a tremendous asset in various aspects of life. I wouldn't have successfully made it this far in life without my spectacularly unique and divergent brain! I have been a problem-solving machine for the past five years, and none of that would have been possible with a normal brain.

Imagine you're planning a birthday party for your child. Instead of sticking to the usual themes, your mind races with ideas—an underwater adventure, a space odyssey, or a jungle safari. Each concept builds upon the last, creating a party that's not just memorable but uniquely yours. This kind of creative problem-solving extends beyond parties. It can manifest in your work, hobbies, and even daily tasks. For example, when faced with a cluttered room, you might envision a completely new layout that maximizes space and functionality, transforming chaos into order.

Hyperfocus, another common trait in ADHD, can lead to remarkable creative breakthroughs. When you're deeply engaged in a task you love, time seems to disappear. Hours can fly by as you immerse yourself in your project, achieving a level of concentration that allows for incredible productivity and innovation. This hyperfocus is not just about intense concentration; it's about being in a state of flow where creativity flourishes. Hyperfocus has allowed me to enter entirely different industries as a novice and hit the ground running. Thanks again for looking out for me, brain!

To harness and nurture your creativity, set aside dedicated time for creative pursuits. Make creative pursuits a regular part of your routine, whether painting, writing, or crafting. Use brainstorming techniques like mind mapping to explore new ideas and see connections that might not be immediately obvious. Engaging in activities that stimulate creative thinking, such as visiting art galleries, reading diverse genres, or even walking in nature, can also fuel your imagination.

Try incorporating daily creativity challenges into your routine. Start your day with a simple exercise: think of ten new uses for an ordinary object, like a paperclip. This exercise warms up your creative muscles and encourages you to see everyday items in a new light. Journaling ideas and reflections can also be a powerful tool. Keep a notebook where you jot down thoughts, sketches, and inspirations. Over time, you'll build a treasure trove of ideas to revisit and develop.

Participating in creative workshops or classes can provide structure and inspiration. Whether it's a painting workshop, a creative writing class, or a photography course, these environments offer opportunities to learn new techniques, meet like-minded individuals, and push the boundaries of your creativity. The sense of community and shared passion can be incredibly motivating and enriching.

I love to create. I wouldn't say I am great at anything in particular, but I love making new things or improving existing ones. DIY and refurbishing projects bring me a lot of joy. Designing garden spaces, greenhouses, flower beds, and planting schedules excites me. Ready for the dorkiest admission ever? I LOVE creating Excel spreadsheets. They sound boring, but I can develop realms of order and organization in Excel that I can only dream of having in real life. My brain thrives on the beauty of a well-organized spreadsheet, and I can only thank my first professional job for this skill set. Seriously, I'm so glad I didn't bail on that interview (Way to go, twenty-year-old Kayla!). Learning fuels my creativity. Nature and exquisite architecture ignite inspiration in me. Reading poetic novels makes my soul soar. Find what sparks life and creativity in you, then prioritize these experiences.

The innate creativity found in individuals with ADHD is not just a trait; it's a superpower. By recognizing and nurturing this creativity, you can turn what might seem like a challenge into a significant strength. Embrace your divergent thinking, celebrate your unique perspective, and let your imagination soar. Creative minds that think differently enrich the world; your ADHD-driven creativity is a gift waiting to bloom.

Empathy and Intuition: Hidden Strengths of ADHD

One evening, I was in a deep conversation with a friend who was going through a tough time. As she shared her feelings, I could almost feel her pain as if it were mine. I listened intently, offering words of comfort and understanding. This ability to deeply connect with others is one of the hidden strengths of ADHD. People with ADHD often have heightened emotional sensitivity, allowing them to pick up on subtle social cues and emotions that others might miss. This gift can make you incredibly empathetic and intuitive, traits that are invaluable in building strong relationships and understanding others.

The connection between ADHD and heightened emotional sensitivity means that you can often sense how others are feeling before they even say a word. This intuition can guide you in making decisions considering the emotional well-being of those around you. For example, you might instinctively know when a colleague needs a break during a stressful project or when a friend needs someone to talk to. Empathy can enhance communication and connection, creating a supportive and understanding environment where people feel valued and heard.

To harness and nurture your empathy and intuition, practice active listening and emotional validation. Active listening means fully concentrating on what the other person is saying rather than planning your response. Show that you're engaged by nodding, maintaining eye contact, and providing verbal affirmations like "I understand" or "That sounds tough." Emotional validation involves acknowledging and accepting someone's feelings without judgment. Phrases like "It's okay to feel that way" or "Your feelings are valid" can make a significant difference.

Trusting and honing your intuitive insights can also be powerful. When you get a gut feeling about a situation or person, take a moment to reflect on it. Your ADHD brain picks up on subtle cues and patterns that normal minds miss, resulting in a finely tuned intuition. Engaging in activities that cultivate empathy, such as volunteering or working with communities in need, can further develop these traits. Volunteering at a local shelter or participating in community outreach programs can provide real-world opportunities to practice empathy and connect with others on a deeper level.

Reflective journaling can be a valuable exercise to enhance your empathy and intuition. Take time each day to write about your empathetic experiences, how you felt, and what you learned from them. This practice can help you become more aware of your emotional responses and improve your ability to connect with others. Mindfulness exercises focused on emotional awareness can also be beneficial. Spend a few minutes daily meditating on your emotions, noticing how they arise and change without trying to alter them. The practice of self-awareness can increase your emotional intelligence and self-awareness.

Role-playing scenarios can be another effective way to practice empathy. Consider situations where you might need to offer support or understand someone's perspective. Role-play these scenarios with a trusted friend or family member, taking turns being the speaker and the listener. This exercise can help you develop the skills to respond empathetically in real-life situations.

By recognizing these hidden strengths of ADHD and actively nurturing them, you can build stronger relationships, create supportive environments, and connect with others on a deeper level. Your heightened emotional sensitivity is not just a trait; it's a superpower that can bring empathy, understanding, and connection into every interaction.

Turning Challenges into Opportunities

One evening, as I sat with a cup of tea, reflecting on my day, I realized how many small obstacles I had navigated. Misplacing my keys, forgetting an appointment, and struggling to focus on a task at work were on the list. These daily challenges, while frustrating, also presented growth opportunities. ADHD can often feel like a series of hurdles, but each can be a stepping stone toward personal growth and success. Reframing challenges as opportunities for learning can transform your perspective and help you develop resilience and adaptability.

Viewing obstacles as opportunities means shifting your mindset. Instead of seeing a missed deadline as a failure, consider it a chance to refine your time management skills. For example, if you've struggled with organization, use that challenge to explore new systems and tools that might work better for you. Embrace the trial-and-error process as a learning experience. Overcoming challenges related to ADHD can foster resilience. Each time you navigate an obstacle, you build a toolkit of strategies and skills to help you handle future difficulties.

"Pressure is a privilege." - Billie Jean King

Resilience and adaptability are often born from adversity. Setbacks strengthen your ability to bounce back and adapt. When you encounter a difficulty, remind yourself that it's a chance to learn and grow. Replace negative thoughts like "I can't do this" with empowering ones like "This is tough, but I can handle it." Cognitive reframing involves looking at a situation from a different perspective. For example, if you struggle with focus, reframe it as an opportunity to discover new techniques that improve your concentration.

Setting realistic goals and celebrating progress are also crucial. Break down larger tasks into smaller, manageable steps. This approach makes goals feel less daunting and provides a sense of accomplishment as you complete each step. Celebrate these small victories, no matter how minor they may seem. Recognizing your progress boosts motivation and reinforces a positive mindset. Seeking support and resources can make a significant difference. Reach out to friends, family, or professionals who understand ADHD and can offer guidance and encouragement. Joining support groups or online communities can provide a sense of belonging and shared experiences.

Engaging in exercises designed to reframe challenges can be incredibly helpful. Start by writing down your challenges and identifying potential opportunities within them. For instance, if you often misplace items, view it as an opportunity to develop better organizational habits. Reflective journaling on past successes and lessons learned can provide valuable insights. Write about times when you overcame obstacles and what strategies worked for you. Visualization exercises can also be powerful. Spend a few minutes each day visualizing positive outcomes. Imagine yourself successfully navigating challenges and achieving your goals.

By reframing obstacles, practicing positive self-talk, setting realistic goals, seeking support, and engaging in reflective exercises, you can leverage your ADHD-related challenges as powerful catalysts for growth. Each challenge you face is an opportunity to learn, adapt, and thrive.

Celebrating Your Spectacular Brain: Stories of Success and Triumph

As I sat in my cozy living room, sipping tea and reflecting on my journey with ADHD, I realized how important it is to celebrate the unique strengths and successes that come with it. Recognizing and celebrating individual achievements can be transformative. It emphasizes the value of self-acceptance and pride. When you acknowledge your triumphs, no matter how small, you reinforce a positive self-image and build confidence that propels you forward.

Reflecting on your achievements is a powerful practice. Start by writing your personal success story. Think about the challenges you've overcome and the strengths you've discovered. Documenting these moments can provide a sense of accomplishment and remind you of your resilience. Creating a "celebration journal" is another effective tool. Dedicate a notebook to recording your achievements, big or small. Each entry becomes a testament to your growth and a source of motivation during tough times.

Practicing gratitude and self-recognition exercises can further enhance your sense of accomplishment. Each day, take a moment to acknowledge something you're proud of. It could be as simple as completing a task on time or as significant as achieving a long-term goal. Regularly practicing gratitude cultivates a positive mindset, focusing on your strengths and successes. To make this practice even more effective, feel the gratitude within you as an emotion. Gratitude is only as powerful as the emotion you create from those grateful thoughts.

I have lived most of my life with a positive mentality and gratitude practice. It was not until I actually felt the emotion of gratitude that I noticed significant improvements in my life. It's one thing to think, "I am so thankful for my bed," and another thing entirely to feel your heart swell in gratitude for a modern object that exponentially improves the quality of life. I find myself overcome with gratitude over the running water in my faucets. Why? Simply because I can imagine what it would be like to be without running water. I can picture the effort required to tote water into a house for drinking, cooking, and flushing toilets. Notice, I didn't even mention hot water. I challenge you to examine ordinary objects in your life. Choose something most people would find ridiculous and practice gratitude. You will be amazed by the abundance of reasons you have to be thankful.

I would love it if you, readers, share your success stories. You could include it in your book review, email it to me, or share it on social media. I want to celebrate with you. There is nothing like a community of like-minded individuals discussing passion and success to spark inspiration in others. Joining ADHD support groups and communities provides a platform to connect with others who understand your experiences. Sharing your stories on social media can inspire and motivate others while fostering a sense of belonging. Participating in public speaking events or writing about your experiences allows you to reach a broader audience, spreading awareness and understanding of ADHD. Consider the impact of sharing your journey with others. Another woman may not give up because she related to your story. One person may find the courage to get the support she has needed her entire life. An entire generation of children could be inspired to be more empathetic to their ADHD classmates because they were raised with awareness of ADHD challenges.

By celebrating the unique strengths and successes of women with ADHD, we create a culture of acceptance and pride. Each achievement, no matter how small, is a step towards recognizing the value of our uniquely spectacular brains. Embrace your accomplishments, share your stories, and inspire others to do the same. Your ADHD is not a hindrance; it's a superpower that can lead to remarkable success and fulfillment. The need for your story exists.

Conclusion

As we end this journey together, let's take a moment to reflect on the purpose and vision of this book. Our primary goal has been to offer simple, actionable solutions for women struggling with ADHD symptoms. We've aimed to encourage you to see ADHD not as a burden but as a unique gift that brings its own advantages. Understanding and embracing your uniquely spectacular brain allows you to navigate life with more confidence and joy.

Throughout the chapters, we've explored various aspects of living with ADHD, from understanding your diagnosis to managing emotions and from organizing your daily routines to leveraging technology. We've delved into how ADHD manifests differently in women, the impact of hormonal changes, and the journey of late diagnosis. Each chapter provided practical strategies and real-life examples to help you navigate these challenges.

We discussed the importance of emotional regulation and self-esteem, introducing tools like Dialectical Behavior Therapy (DBT) and self-compassion exercises. We explored time management techniques, the power of brain dumps, and strategies to overcome procrastination. Enhancing focus and productivity was another critical area where we looked at harnessing hyperfocus, using body doubling, and creating distraction-free environments.

In relationships, we examined effective communication with partners, navigating friendships, and building a supportive network. We also touched on career and professional life, emphasizing creativity, time management, and self-advocacy. Holistic health and well-being were covered, with insights into nutrition, exercise, earthing, meditation, mindfulness, and self-care routines. For those of you who are parents, we provided strategies for balancing parenting duties and managing sensory overload.

Key takeaways from this book include the understanding that ADHD is a multifaceted condition that affects various aspects of life. However, you can turn these challenges into opportunities with the right tools and strategies. Recognizing and celebrating your strengths, whether they're creativity, empathy, or hyperfocus, can transform how you view yourself and your ADHD.

Self-compassion and empowerment are crucial. It's vitally important to understand and accept yourself, embracing ADHD as a unique part of who you are. Transitioning your mindset reveals the true journey isn't about fixing yourself but discovering and leveraging your strengths. Treat yourself with the kindness and understanding you would offer a dear friend.

I implore you to implement the strategies and exercises discussed in this book. Take small steps towards creating routines, managing time, and enhancing focus. Join support groups, engage with online communities, and seek professional help as required. Your journey with ADHD is unique, and you have the power to shape it positively.

Remember, you are not alone. Many women share in your experiences and challenges. With the right mindset and tools, you can thrive. Embrace the journey of self-discovery and growth. Celebrate your achievements, no matter how small, and recognize the progress you make each day. Your ADHD brain is not a hindrance but a source of incredible potential and strength.

Thank you for taking the time to read this book. Your effort to improve your life and embrace your ADHD traits is commendable. It's been an honor to share this journey with you, and I hope the insights and strategies provided here have been helpful.

In closing, celebrate your unique brain. Embrace the journey ahead with confidence and hope. You have the tools, the strength, and the support to create a balanced, fulfilling life. Your ADHD is a part of you, and it contributes to the spectacular person you are. Here's to your journey of self-discovery and growth.

PS - If you find me overly optimistic and disgustingly cheesy, please know that it is the result of experiencing a truly magical life through the spectacular gifts ADHD has given me. I genuinely think and speak this way. I know your struggles, and I am convinced you will have the life you deserve once you realize the overflowing power within you. If I can figure it out, you can too.

Your brain was made for this!

Xoxo,

Kayla

You've Got This!

Empower Someone Else with Your Review

Now that you've got the tools to embrace your ADHD and celebrate your unique brain, it's time to share your journey and help others find the same support. Overcoming feelings of unworthiness, inadequacy, and low self-esteem is a tall order. If the information in this book helped you achieve those goals, please share your story with others.

By leaving your honest review on Amazon, you'll guide other women with ADHD to the resources they need, helping them feel understood and empowered, just like you.

Thank you for being part of this journey. Our knowledge grows when we share it, and you're helping me spread that knowledge further.

Scan the QR below to leave your review on Amazon.

References

- *Gender differences in adult ADHD: Cognitive function ...* https://www.ncbi.nlm.nih.gov/pmc/articles/PMC7561166/

- *Study: Women with Undiagnosed ADHD Suffer Poor Self ...* https://www.additudemag.com/adhd-symptoms-adult-women-undiagnosed/

- *ADHD and Hormonal Changes in Women* https://www.healthline.com/health/adhd/adhd-and-hormonal-changes-in-women

- *Women Leaders with ADHD: Inspiring Success Stories* https://www.additudemag.com/women-leaders-with-adhd/

- *DBT for ADHD: Why Dialectical Behavior Therapy Works* https://www.additudemag.com/dbt-for-adhd-dialectical-behavioral-therapy/

- *ADHD and Self-Esteem: What's the Connection?* https://www.healthline.com/health/adhd/adhd-and-self-esteem

- *Cognitive-behavioural interventions for attention deficit ...* https://www.ncbi.nlm.nih.gov/pmc/articles/PMC6494390/

- *Silver linings of ADHD: a thematic analysis of adults ...* https://www.ncbi.nlm.nih.gov/pmc/articles/PMC10551976/

- *ADHD Time Blindness: How to Detect It & Regain Control …* https://add.org/adhd-time-blindness/

- *The Power of a Brain Dump: How to Untangle Your ADHD …* https://www.neverdefeatedcoaching.net/the-power-of-a-brain-dump-how-to-untangle-your-adhd-mind/

- *5 Strategies to Make and Keep Routines With Adult ADHD* https://www.psychologytoday.com/us/blog/your-way-adhd/202211/5-strategies-make-and-keep-routines-adult-adhd

- *Stop ADHD Procrastination: Getting Things Done* https://www.additudemag.com/stop-adhd-procrastination/

- *Hyperfocus Symptoms: The Good, the Bad, and the Ugly* https://www.additudemag.com/hyperfocus-symptoms-positives-negatives-strategies/

- *Body Doubling for ADHD: What Is It and How Does It Work?* https://www.healthline.com/health/adhd/body-double-adhd

- Tolle, E. (1997). *The Power of Now: A Guide to Spiritual Enlightenment.* Novato, CA: New World Library.

- Wagner, C. (2019). A journey to mindfulness: Eckhart Tolle and *The Power of Now. Journal of Transpersonal Psychology, 51*(1), 22-39.

- Yonge, R. (2014). Mindfulness and spiritual practice: Reflections on Eckhart Tolle's teachings. *Mindfulness Journal, 5*(2), 121-135.

- *How to Practice Mindfulness with ADHD: Meditation for …* https://www.additudemag.com/how-to-practice-mindfulness-adhd/

- *Adult ADHD at Work: Tips for Organization and Control - WebMD* https://www.webmd.com/add-adhd/adhd-in-the-workplace#:~:text=Personal%20space.,conference%20room%20or%20a%20cubicle.

- *Marriage Communication Tips for Spouses of ADHD Adults* https://www.additudemag.com/marriage-communication-tips-adhd-spouses/

- *ADHD in Women: Lived Experiences, Real-Life Stories* https://www.additudemag.com/slideshows/adhd-in-women-lived-experiences/

- *How to Make Friends: Advice for Women with ADHD* https://www.additudemag.com/how-to-make-friends-adhd-women/

- *Lifestyle Supports for Women with ADHD* https://chadd.org/for-adults/lifestyle-supports-for-women-with-adhd/

- *The Creativity of ADHD* https://www.scientificamerican.com/article/the-creativity-of-adhd/

- *Girl Power(houses): Inspiring Women with ADHD* https://www.additudemag.com/famous-women-with-adhd-work/

- *Time Management Skills for ADHD Brains: Practical Advice* https://www.additudemag.com/time-management-skills-adhd-brain/

- *The Importance of Self-Advocacy for Women with ADHD* https://www.hacksandknacks.com/self-advocacy-for-women-with-adhd/

- *ADHD Diet For Adults: Foods to Eat and Avoid - ADDA* https://add.org/adhd-diet/

- Sarris, J., Kean, J., Schweitzer, I., & Lake, J. (2011). Complementary medicines (herbal and nutritional products) in the treatment of Attention Deficit Hyperactivity Disorder (ADHD): a systematic review of the evidence. Complementary Therapies in Medicine.

- Arnold, L. E., DiSilvestro, R. A., Bozzolo, D., et al. (2011). Zinc for ADHD: placebo-controlled double-blind pilot study of zinc supplementation. Journal of Child and Adolescent Psychopharmacology.

- Bélanger, S. A., & Hutchinson, J. (2005). Nutrition and ADHD: review of the evidence. Canadian Journal of Dietetic Practice and Research.

- Faraone, S. V., Banaschewski, T., Coghill, D., et al. (2021). The World Federation of ADHD International Consensus Statement: 208 Evidence-based Conclusions about the Disorder. Neuroscience & Biobehavioral Reviews.

- Gow, R. V., Hibbeln, J. R., & Omega-3 Fatty Acid Research. (2014). Omega-3 fatty acids for attention-deficit hyperactivity disorder. Current Psychiatry Reports

- Chandrasekhar, K., et al. (2012). "A prospective, randomized double-blind, placebo-controlled study of safety and efficacy of a high-concentration full-spectrum extract of Ashwagandha root in reducing stress and anxiety in adults." *Indian Journal of Psychological Medicine.*

- Pratte, M. A., et al. (2014). "An alternative treatment for anxiety: A systematic review of human trials testing the anxiolytic effects of Ashwagandha." *Journal of Clinical Psychiatry.*

- Chandrasekhar, K., et al. (2012). "A prospective, randomized double-blind, placebo-controlled study of safety and efficacy of a high-concentration full-spectrum extract of Ashwagandha root in reducing stress and anxiety in adults." *Indian Journal of Psychological Medicine.*

- Olsson, E. M., et al. (2009). "A randomized double-blind placebo-controlled study of the effects of Rhodiola rosea on mental performance, physical capacity, and stress response." *Phytomedicine.*

- https://www.thecarlatreport.com/blogs/2-the-carlat-psychiatry-podcast/post/4567-four-natural-therapies-for-adhd-with-richard

-brown

- Panossian, A., et al. (2010). "Adaptogens in mental and behavioral disorders." *Psychiatry Research.*

- Reay, J. L., et al. (2005). "Effects of Panax ginseng, Ginkgo biloba, and their combination on cognitive performance and mood." *Physiology & Behavior.*

- Kennedy, D. O., et al. (2001). "Improved cognitive performance and mental fatigue following a single dose of Ginseng." *Journal of Psychopharmacology.*

- *Exercise and ADHD: How Physical Activity Boosts Your Brain* https://www.additudemag.com/exercise-and-the-adhd-brain/

- *How to Practice Mindfulness with ADHD: Meditation for ...* https://www.additudemag.com/how-to-practice-mindfulness-adhd/

- *ADHD Stress Management and Coping Skills: Self-Care ...* https://www.additudemag.com/slideshows/adhd-stress-management-skills-for-adults/

- *How to Parent with ADHD: Parenting Skills & Strategies* https://www.additudemag.com/parenting-with-adhd-strategies/

- *ADHD & Sensory Overload: Managing Overstimulation* https://add.org/sensory-overload-adhd/#:~:text=Learning%20relaxation%20methods%2C%20like%20yoga,while%20reading%20and%20sipping%20tea.

- *The Efficacy of Visual Activity Schedule Intervention in ... - NCBI* https://www.ncbi.nlm.nih.gov/pmc/articles/PMC8733412/#:~:text=The%20visual%20activity%20schedule%20(VAS,classroom%20skills%2C%20and%20academic%20skills.

- *The Best Digital Calendar Habits for ADHD* https://habitsandhome

- .com/the-best-digital-calendar-habits-for-adhd/

- *Budgeting Tips That Work for ADHD Brains* https://www.additudemag.com/budgeting-tips-for-adhd-brains/

- *Why You Should Automate Bill Payments* https://www.regions.com/insights/personal/personal-finances/creating-a-financial-plan/online-banking-automate-bill-payments

- *12 Ways to Resist Impulse Buying: ADHD Shopping Secrets* https://www.additudemag.com/impulse-buying-money-problems-adhd-adults/

- *Managing Money and ADHD: Expenses and Goals* https://chadd.org/for-adults/managing-money-and-adhd-expenses-and-goals/

- *ADHD sensory overload: Causes, treatment, and more* https://www.medicalnewstoday.com/articles/adhd-sensory-overload

- *Sneaky Sensory Triggers in ADHD That No One Talks About* https://www.psychologytoday.com/us/blog/the-reality-gen-z/202112/sneaky-sensory-triggers-in-adhd-no-one-talks-about

- *Creating an ADHD-Friendly Home Environment* https://www.northmetropsych.com/blog/k99ypml8et6x5m6m4cdxafshnyp56p

- *The Ultimate List of Sensory Products for Adults* https://harkla.co/blogs/special-needs/sensory-products-adults?srsltid=AfmBOooj5XyNgj87HB71etTNsqhUC1nLVUTcYLJ8aKZSbJ_RgxAFUKNj

- *Best Productivity Apps for Adults with ADHD: Our Top Picks* https://www.additudemag.com/best-productivity-apps-adhd-adults/

- https://www.busybudgeter.com/simple-budget-categories/

- *How Digital Planner Apps can Help Adults with ADHD - Tiimo* https://www.tiimoapp.com/blog/digital-planner-apps-for-adhd#:~:text=The%20Power%20of%20Digital%20Planners,-%E2%80%8D&text=A%20key%20feature%20of%20these,easier%20to%20see%20and%20remember.

- *Best Mental Health Apps for ADHD* https://www.additudemag.com/slideshows/best-mental-health-apps-for-adhd-headspace-talkspace-better-help/

- Dispenza, J. (2013). *Breaking the habit of being yourself: How to lose your mind and create a new one.* Hay House LLC.

- Dispenza, J. (2015). *You are the placebo: Making your mind matter.* Hay House LLC.

- Dispenza, J. (2019). *Becoming supernatural: How common people are doing the uncommon.* Hay House UK Ltd.

- *https://www.facebook.com/share/v/tLmRAkE8DC39ZLBp/*

- *https://itsadhdfriendly.com/dr-joe-dispenza/ and https://youtu.be/43V7ab-_NVs*

- Harper, A. (2024). *30-day executive functioning skills mastery for adults with ADHD: A practical guide with real-life solutions to strengthen executive functioning skills in 30 days or less and thrive with ADHD.* Plural Creations.

- Dawson, P., & Guare, R. (2009). *Smart but scattered: The revolutionary "executive skills" approach to helping kids reach their potential.* Guilford Press.

- Brown, R., Chevalier, G., & Hill, M. (2015). Grounding after moderate eccentric contractions reduces muscle damage. *Open Access Journal of Sports Medicine, 6,* 305-317. https://doi.org/10.2147/OAJSM.S84947

- Chevalier, G., Sinatra, S. T., Oschman, J. L., Sokal, K., & Sokal, P. (2015). Earthing: Health implications of reconnecting the human body to the Earth's surface electrons. *Journal of Environmental and Public Health*, 2012. https://doi.org/10.1155/2012/291541

- Ghaly, M., & Teplitz, D. (2004). The biologic effects of grounding the human body during sleep as measured by cortisol levels and subjective reporting of sleep, pain, and stress. *The Journal of Alternative and Complementary Medicine*, 10(5), 767-776. https://doi.org/10.1089/acm.2004.10.767

- Oschman, J. L. (2007). *Energy medicine: The scientific basis*. Churchill Livingstone.

- Sokal, K., & Sokal, P. (2011). Earthing the human body influences physiologic processes. *Journal of Alternative and Complementary Medicine*, 17(4), 301-308. https://doi.org/10.1089/acm.2010.0687

- *ADDA Virtual Peer Support Groups for Adults with ADHD* https://add.org/adda-virtual-programs/

- *The Link Between Creativity and ADHD* https://www.psychologytoday.com/us/blog/mythbusting-adhd/202205/the-link-between-creativity-and-adhd

- *Women Leaders with ADHD: Inspiring Success Stories* https://www.additudemag.com/women-leaders-with-adhd/

- *Unlocking the Power of the ADHD Empath* https://www.goblinxadhd.com/blog/unlocking-the-power-of-the-adhd-empath-navigating/

- *Turning Challenges from ADHD into Strengths* https://www.ldonline.org/ld-topics/adhd/turning-challenges-adhd-strengths

Made in the USA
Las Vegas, NV
06 January 2025

4ed7a576-63ca-45e2-ad70-1c86a9fc7b61R01